# GOOD ENERGY

Renewable Power and
the Design of Everyday Life

# GOOD ENERGY

Jared Green

PRINCETON ARCHITECTURAL PRESS · NEW YORK

# Table of Contents

# Foreword:
# Renewable Energy Can't Be Separate

—

by Walter Hood

The Solar Pergola, which opened in 2004, was designed by Martínez Lapeña-Torres Arquitectos, a Barcelona-based architecture firm, with Phönix SonnenStrom AG, a solar energy system engineering firm. The canopy, which provides a platform for 2,668 monocrystalline PV panels with a capacity of 449 kilowatts, spans 367 by 164 feet (112 by 50 meters), an area equivalent in size to a soccer field. The canopy is tilted 35 degrees to the south in order to optimize the PV panels' sun exposure. Reaching a height of 177 feet (54 meters), the Solar Pergola provides shade for public events while also meeting the energy needs of 150 families and avoiding some 440 tons of carbon dioxide emissions annually.

**How do you take a standard technology— the photovoltaic (PV) panel—and design it to become something more?**

Consider a large array of PV panels. They are beautiful just as they are. Aggregated together, they have this visual power. But through design, a beautiful aggregation of PV panels can express something greater than just renewable energy. Instead of treating PV panels only as objects, we can integrate them into the built environment so they become something more. They can speak to place and ecology.

In the US, individualism, to a certain degree, goes against the collective. Bravado about using oil goes deeper in our culture than we think. It is about driving the big truck instead of the small car.

For many decades, renewable energy was seen as making us weaker. Remember the 1980s? We essentially passed our solar energy science on to Germany. After Ronald Reagan became president, he removed the PV panels President Jimmy Carter had put on the White House roof. As a country, we thought, "Yeah, we don't need renewable energy."

After we [Hood Design Studio] designed the Solar Strand, a quarter-mile-long array of PV panels at the University at Buffalo in Buffalo, New York, in 2012 (see page 148), I was invited to present at a European conference on solar energy. In parts of Europe, such as Germany, designers and engineers are incorporating PV panels in noise-canceling walls along freeways running north-south. Renewable energy has become culturally acceptable in Europe because these systems are highly integrated into daily life.

What the Europeans have shown us is that renewable energy cannot be considered extra. Too often, we think about renewable energy in design today as an add-on. But in other cultures, renewable energy has become part of the native language. In these places, people no longer say, "If it costs more, we don't do it." Renewable energy is ingrained.

When I first saw the Solar Pergola at the Universal Forum of Cultures on the waterfront in Barcelona, I was excited. You read the frame for the panels as a giant pergola, but it is actually a huge energy collector. It is sculptural and a beautiful piece of design.

The message of the Solar Pergola is that renewable energy needs to be beautiful and inspire. People need to look at a pergola or a home that integrates renewable energy and say, "I want one of those!" As designers, we need to try to get folks to say that. We need to design ways in which renewable energy can be integrated into all aspects of daily life.

Lars Lerup, one of my professors in architecture school, designed a house called Villa Prima Facie. In this project, Lerup understood that the south wall of a house, which receives the fullest sun exposure, is a "hot" wall. The north wall, which receives the least sun exposure during the day, is a "cold" wall. This suggests energy can be generated through PV panels on the south side of houses and apartment buildings. A simple approach like this gives us new ways of thinking about how to orient and build homes.

When I first moved to Berkeley in the late 1980s, solar water heaters had already been incorporated on the roofs of houses and apartment buildings. Arriving from the East Coast, this was completely new to me. I thought, "Wow, every building has these." These systems were wonderful, because I never had to worry about whether there was enough hot water, and I didn't have to pay a water bill.

Then I moved to Oakland, California, and it was completely different. When I look at PV arrays on roofs today, they are still not commonplace. When you see rooftop PVs, they seem unique.

Integration has to be the way. At the opening of the Solar Strand, people asked me, "How do you let people in there and go up to PV panels?" I responded: "What do you mean?" I learned that most people thought if they touched a PV panel, they were going to get shocked. There was a perception that PV panels need to be separate.

At Solar Strand, we put all the electric cables and conduits into pipes. It cost extra, but it allows people to become part of the experience of renewable energy—and that is my big goal. As long as things are separate, we don't take them into consideration. But if renewable energy is integrated into our daily patterns, it will no longer be special. I do think that is divine.

You may have seen those light posts with a small PV panel attached. The PV panel powers the street light. A designer might look at that panel and street light and come up with new approach that integrates the PV into the structure of the light itself. For a long time, architects looked at a PV panel and then looked at the building and would put the panel on the building. Now PV panels have become the facade. This is what I am getting at—this is where design matters.

We also have huge horizontal pieces of ground surface in our communities that can be put to use.

It is hard to imagine this today, but, as far as sun exposure, the ground is no different from a roof. We can think of the ground as a solar collector. We can create solar paving. We have to think about all the impervious space we have in a new way, which, again, is where design comes in.

This is our choice as designers. We cannot accept that the way things are now is just part of the soup. We have got to make the soup.

In *Good Energy*, you'll find 35 great projects from around the world that are doing just that. The projects in this book demonstrate the ability of design to integrate renewable energy into our daily life.

*Walter Hood is an artist, landscape designer, and educator. He is creative director and founder of Hood Design Studio in Oakland, California, and a professor of landscape architecture, environmental planning, and urban design at the University of California at Berkeley. He lectures on professional and theoretical projects nationally and internationally. Hood is a recipient of the 2017 Academy of Arts and Letters Architecture Award, 2019 Knight Public Spaces Fellowship, 2019 MacArthur Fellowship, and 2019 Dorothy and Lillian Gish Prize.*

To make Solar Strand safe and accessible to the public, Hood Design Studio inserted electrical cables for the PVs into low steel pipes on either side of the central pathway between the racks of panels. The pipes were also designed to work as footrests and seats.

During an educational tour, University at Buffalo students were invited to see firsthand that they wouldn't be shocked by touching Solar Strand's PV panels. The silicon PV panels, which are engineered to withstand extreme temperature and weather, get hotter or colder depending on ambient air temperature and the amount of sunlight.

# Introduction

Good design makes products, services, and systems feel natural, even indispensable. Think of your favorite chair, restaurant, or website, how it feels made just for you. Now imagine what a similar attachment to renewable energy would feel like: the pride one has for a comfortable, healthy home run on 100 percent clean power.

Design can help speed and improve the shift to renewable energy by making life with clean power easy, appealing, and affordable. The more desirable renewable energy becomes, the more people will want it in their daily lives.

With existing technologies and models, it's possible to create single-family homes and residential communities, office buildings, schools, and public spaces to meet or even exceed their own energy needs. This can be accomplished by incorporating PV panels, wind turbines, and geothermal systems; orienting and optimizing buildings for solar exposure; electrifying building systems, including those for heating, cooling, and ventilation; and storing and managing energy on-site through batteries and energy-management systems. The challenge is pulling all of these systems together in a way that generates the emotional attachment good design does.

For those concerned about any negative impacts of wind, solar, or geothermal power plants, good planning and design can change minds. Power-generation facilities don't have to be eyesores that simply generate electricity. They can instead be planned and designed to be beautiful, environmentally sensitive, and to provide access to affordable renewable energy that offers significant benefits.

One benefit worth highlighting: Renewable energy can make us more resilient to climate impacts. The generation of electricity from renewable sources is highly decentralized. Clean electricity is now being produced within our communities—through large and small power plants, across our rooftops, and in our community spaces.

This approach greatly strengthens communities' resilience to heat waves, wildfires, and hurricanes that now regularly disrupt centralized power infrastructure. Furthermore, all communities—especially historically underserved and marginalized communities—can not only benefit from these systems but also increasingly participate in their design and construction, developing skills that lead to well-paying green jobs.

Design is a pathway for bringing renewable energy into people's daily lives—and a way to make the transformation more inclusive and equitable. Approximately 80 to 85 percent of the world's population lives in developing countries, which account for nearly two-thirds of the world's greenhouse gas emissions. Affordable building models that can work in every climate and income level are incredibly important given that the world population is expected to increase to 11.2 billion by 2100 and that we can expect thousands of new cities to form in developing countries in coming decades.

An estimated 1.5 to 2 billion new homes will be needed by the end of the century. It's essential that those new buildings not only generate their own power but also store carbon and be healthier, more affordable, and more beautiful. New and retrofitted buildings must be more sustainable and resilient to climate impacts at lower costs while providing a better living experience. Architects and designers have to show what that better experience looks and feels like so these improved approaches spread rapidly around the globe.

### The Big Picture: The Time for Transformation Is Now

A 2018 report from the United Nations Intergovernmental Panel on Climate Change (IPCC) states that we have precious little time—a decade or so—to phase out fossil-fuel use; integrate renewable energy into our homes, offices, and transportation systems; and build thousands of new clean power plants. We can only put another 420 gigatons of greenhouse gas emissions into the atmosphere if we want a good chance of meeting the most ambitious goals of the 2015 Paris Climate Accord, which is keeping global temperature increase to 1.5 degrees Celsius (2.7 degrees Fahrenheit), instead of 2 degrees Celsius (3.6 degrees Fahrenheit). At our current pace, our carbon budget will be used up by 2030.

To date, global temperatures have increased 1 degree Celsius (1.8 degrees Fahrenheit) above preindustrial levels. The IPCC argues that limiting warming to just another half a degree Celsius will still have adverse global impacts but will at least stave off some of the worst effects and make a major difference for several hundred million people. Achieving the 1.5 degree Celsius limit, a key target outlined in the accord, needs to happen in the very near term, so we cannot delay. The IPCC states that if humanity can achieve net-zero emissions in the coming few decades, additional warming could essentially be halted.

A majority of populations sampled in 40 countries by the Pew Research Center understand the scale of the issues and think climate change is a "very serious problem." Many feel a deep sense of urgency to move away from fossil fuels and to decarbonize their lives. Young people, in particular, demand an immediate acceleration in the transition to renewable energy, as they will bear the brunt of a far less hospitable future.

In 2018, Swedish student Greta Thunberg, then in ninth grade, organized peaceful strikes in front of the Swedish Parliament, calling for Sweden to dramatically reduce its greenhouse gas emissions and meet its obligations under the Paris Climate Accord. Inspiring a global protest movement among students of all ages, a youth coalition coordinated a series of escalating actions that culminated in a September 20, 2019, protest with an estimated 4 million students taking part in 4,500 events worldwide. One of their key demands: an end to fossil fuels and a transition to 100 percent renewable energy as soon as possible.

The IPCC report outlines potential pathways to net-zero emissions. Greenhouse gas emissions must decrease by 45 percent from 2010 levels by 2030 and 100 percent by 2050. This requires "rapid and far-reaching transitions in energy, land,urban, and infrastructure (including transport and buildings), and industrial systems." And to underscore, the significant emission reductions needed can only be achieved through a transition to renewable energy.

The Center for Energy and Climate Solutions found that in 2017, just 10.6 percent of total end-use energy—which comprises electricity generation, energy use in vehicles, and building heating and cooling energy—is from renewable sources, such as wind, solar, geothermal, hydropower, and biological sources. While these numbers have grown over the past few decades, greater progress must be made over the next decade if we are to reach a net-zero emission world by 2050.

The IPCC report estimates the damage of a 1.5 degree Celsius increase to the global economy to be tens of trillions of dollars a year as soon as 2040. To avoid the most serious impacts, some US$2.4 trillion a year must be invested in renewable energy through 2035, which would be about 2.5 percent of global gross domestic product annually. This level of investment could create millions of new green jobs worldwide. At the same time, the world must wean itself off fossil fuels.

While we decarbonize electricity, there also needs to be a dramatic increase in the retrofitting of existing buildings to become net-zero at least in terms of their energy use, and all new buildings must be at least net-zero energy moving forward. We also have an obligation to reduce emissions from transportation systems by greatly increasing the market share for affordable EVs.

Think of other economic and social transformations of recent history: the complete overhaul of the US economy during World War II, the incredible growth of the app-based economy since the rise of apps in the mid-2000s. With political will and investment, this new energy transformation is possible.

In a number of regions and countries, political will is taking the form of Green New Deal–style government investments in decarbonization and green-job development. In early 2020, the European Union enacted a Green Deal to achieve carbon neutrality by 2050 through a commitment to leverage €1 trillion (US$1.11 trillion) in public and private investment, along with the creation of a €100 billion (US$111 billion) "just transition fund" to help coal-reliant countries better make the transition to clean energy.

In South Korea, the seventh largest producer of greenhouse gas emissions in the world, President Moon Jae-in made a commitment in 2020 to achieve net-zero emissions by 2050. His administration recently proposed a broad Green New Deal that will include a carbon tax and a down payment on a larger investment package, starting with the allocation of US $10.5 billion over two years to create 133,000 new green jobs in building remodeling, urban forestry, and recycling.

And in the US, there are a number of Green New Deal proposals, which range in cost from $2 trillion to $16.3 trillion over the next decade. A 2019 poll by NPR and PBS NewsHour found that 63 percent of the US population supports some form of public climate investment and regulation to reduce greenhouse gas emissions.

However, according to the Climate Policy Initiative, an analytical and advisory organization, global public and private investment to mitigate or adapt to climate change was only an estimated US$579 billion in 2018, far short of the US$2.4 trillion per year the IPCC identified as needed. Also, developed countries, which pledged to provide US$100 billion in climate aid each year to developing countries as part of the 2015 Paris Climate agreement, are consistently falling short in the funds they deliver.

### How to Bring More People on Board: Focus on the Health Benefits of Renewable Energy

During the COVID-19 pandemic, one fear is that the climate crisis will get lost due to the focus on immediate health concerns. But what the pandemic has shown us is that the environment and human health are deeply connected. Furthermore, low-income communities and historically underserved and marginalized communities with limited access to healthcare, clean air, and green space experience adverse health impacts at a disproportionately higher rate. If our ecosystems and climate are unhealthy and out of balance, humanity is also experiencing negative impacts, with some communities impacted more than others.

Renewable energy is often labeled clean power because it has few of the environmental or health externalities that polluting fossil fuels have. As such, an important theme running through *Good Energy* is the incredible health benefits of integrating renewable energy so that everyone in society can access it.

In the near term, combining a complete transition to renewable-energy sources with the electrification of our society and economy would also save the vast majority of the estimated 7 million people whose lives are cut short by air pollution each year. It could also help the millions more who are sickened or disabled by poor air quality.

According to Mark Z. Jacobson, a professor of civil and environmental engineering at Stanford University, who is interviewed in the next section of this book, if coal, oil, and gas energy infrastructure was replaced with wind, water, and solar, and fossil-fuel-powered vehicles were replaced with clean EVs, we would avoid some US$30 trillion in annual health costs worldwide in 2050. According to the World Bank, air pollution already costs the world US$225 billion in lost labor income and US$5 trillion in welfare losses each year, with the higher burden falling on developing countries and low-income communities in the developed world.

Over the coming decades, if we are unable to keep temperatures from rising less than 1.5 degrees Celsius (2.7 degrees Fahrenheit), we are, scientists assert, in for a future with much higher levels of risk. There will be more flooding, wildfires, extreme heat, sea-level rise, drought, and expanding disease vectors. These all have significant public-health implications.

According to scenarios outlined in a 2019 study in the scientific journal *Nature*, a 2 degree Celsius (3.6 degree Fahrenheit) temperature increase could lead to longer and more powerful heat waves that could impact up to 5.9 billion people worldwide each year while also significantly reducing economic and agricultural activity across warming regions. Water stress could impact up to 3.65 billion people. The initial conflict that fueled the Syrian civil war has been linked with extreme drought. Imagine that violence multiplied, on a global scale. Global migration caused by rising sea levels, wildfires, extreme heat, flooding, and drought could displace thousands of communities, destroying their identity and cultural heritage in the process.

The incredibly diverse global climate-action movement—including those focused on climate and environmental justice, ecological conservation and restoration, sustainable buildings, and fossil-fuels divestment, among many other issues—all have the same goal, which is to bring more people on board. To do that, it is critically important to clearly show the health benefits, in the near- and long-term, of the renewable-energy transformation.

According to Gina McCarthy, former administrator of the Environmental Protection Agency who gave a keynote at the American Society of Landscape Architects' Conference on Landscape Architecture in 2019, what people relate to is "the health and well-being of their children and grandchildren. Health is the best way to get people to care about climate change. Communications must be personal, and health is incredibly personal. Focusing on health impacts will create action."

## Accelerating the Transformation with Good Design

As citizens, our actions build support for greater public and private investment in renewable energy and bolster political will to accelerate the pace of the transformation. There are lots of ways to encourage these changes, including voting for candidates who support climate action, purchasing sustainable products and services or not purchasing much at all, lobbying representatives, boycotting and divesting from companies, protesting, and demanding that clean power mandates be ratcheted up and incentives increased. And *Good Energy* demonstrates that, at the same time, design at all scales—from the single-family house and the office to schools and the power plant—can help build support for integrating renewable power into our built environments.

The book begins with a wide-ranging interview with Mark Z. Jacobson, director of the Atmosphere/Energy program at Stanford University, who explains the many benefits of a shift to 100 percent renewable energy. Jacobson, a scientist who offers a vision inspiring in its depth and scale, explains how all the pieces fit together.

*Good Energy* then offers 35 best-practice models for integrating renewable energy into our built environment. There are models for different climates and income levels in the United States, Europe, Asia, the Middle East, and sub-Saharan Africa.

In Power Homes, there are 15 single-family houses, apartment complexes, and residential communities that show that climate-responsible living can be made affordable for everyone. Projects were selected for their ability to meet or exceed their own energy needs through on-site renewable-energy and energy-efficiency strategies. But what makes many of these projects stand out is how they also incorporate nature to create a sense of health and well-being.

One particularly exciting project in this section, SMA x ECO TOWN Harumidai in Sakai City, Japan, is a walkable, energy-positive, prefabricated community surrounded by a forest. Residents use dashboards inside their houses to earn points for reducing their energy use, which can be redeemed in free rides in shared EVs. Gamification is harnessed for social and environmental good. It's easy to see this model spreading.

Power Community Spaces explores five projects that exemplify how transportation infrastructure and public spaces, including parks and sports centers, are critical to the renewable-energy transformation. If we want more drivers in EVs, we need to use good system design to make EV charging fast, easy, and affordable. Parks and sports centers are places where we express our communal values. They can be designed to generate energy, sending an important signal about our shared environmental values.

Amager Bakke, colloquially known as CopenHill in Copenhagen, Denmark, is a waste-to-energy power plant topped with a park and sports center, with nature areas, hiking trails, and a year-round ski slope. This multifunctional community infrastructure, which has quickly become a landmark and tourist destination, presents a model for public space in the era of climate change.

In Power Education, you can learn about five schools and universities around the world that use their buildings to educate students, teachers, staff, and the community about the value of integrating renewable energy. Healthy, inclusive, energy-positive campuses and educational buildings teach young people the importance of environmental stewardship.

In Lavale, India, the Avasara Academy, which provides scholarships to underprivileged Indian girls, sets an impressive new benchmark for achieving nearly net-zero energy use through low-cost natural technologies paired with PV panels. Harnessing the thermodynamics of warm and cool air, the building uses a "solar chimney" to cool classrooms and dormitories in the tropics. Students are very proud of the sustainable and resilient features of their campus.

Power Offices details five commercial, governmental, and institutional buildings that not only meet or exceed their own energy needs through renewable energy and inventive energy-efficiency strategies but also store carbon and improve employee satisfaction, health, and well-being. Given the amount of office space worldwide could grow 40 percent by 2050, policymakers, planners, and building owners need to apply these sustainable models moving forward.

A significant portion of the Bullitt Center in Seattle, Washington, designed with the ambitious goal of being the most sustainable office building in the world, is made of structural timber sustainably harvested from local forests. The six-story building, which is designed to last 250 years, meets all its own energy and water needs while storing 545 tons of carbon dioxide in its frame.

Finally, in Power Plants, five fascinating examples of geothermal, hydro, solar, and wind power facilities put to rest NIMBY concerns about generating electricity from renewable sources. Renewable power plants, which are absolutely necessary to achieving our climate goals, are designed to provide inclusive access to affordable energy, support ecological regeneration, offer more community amenities, and improve local resilience to the impacts of climate change.

An essay from Björk Guðmundsdóttir, a landscape architect with Landsvirkjun, Iceland's national power company, walks through her company's renewable-energy design policy, which is one of the most progressive in the world. After public backlash over the environmental impact of a hydropower project, Landsvirkjun redesigned its approach to renewable-energy infrastructure projects. Utility-scale hydropower and geothermal projects are now designed in harmony with the landscape. Geothermal and hydropower plants in planning stages show how to marry infrastructure with landscape design, ecological restoration, and placemaking. One planned power plant even includes a hotel and spa.

*Good Energy* offers the reader a much deeper understanding of what renewable energy is and how it works, how it can be incorporated into homes and communities, and how designing with renewable energy improves human health and that of the planet. It's worth noting that many images featured in the book were selected to provide a peek under the hood, so to speak, and demystify these new building systems. Curious about what a mechanical ventilation heat recovery system looks like? Or a home EV charger? Or a chilled beam heating and cooling system? *Good Energy* shows you.

### What Motivates the Designers and Builders of Our New Net-Zero World

As I spent a year talking with optimistic designers, developers, and policy advocates, I kept hearing a few recurring messages that can guide the next steps of communities, policymakers, architects, engineers, planners, and landscape architects:

First, net-zero energy and energy-positive communities aren't that difficult to achieve and don't need to be more expensive than the current status quo. They just require a bit of extra planning and openness to trying out new approaches. Policy and regulatory obstacles slow progress in the near term but are being overcome as cities and local governments enact ambitious new net-zero-policy frameworks.

Instead of mining and processing steel, stone, and concrete and transporting them over long distances, replace much of those materials with local, sustainably harvested structural wood that stores carbon or reuse waste materials. According to the nonprofit organization Architecture 2030, as more buildings become net-zero or even energy-positive operationally, the embodied carbon found within buildings will grow in importance.

Net-zero energy and energy-positive residential communities are also the result of financial innovations that lower the cost of annual energy use for homeowners and renters. Because these projects offer greater environmental and health benefits at lower cost, these developments seem to sell or rent out rapidly. There is a sense of a huge untapped demand from homeowners and renters who care about the environment and their health.

By continuously bringing in outside air, net-zero and energy-positive buildings reduce energy use and improve the health and well-being of occupants while also possibly lowering the risk of exposure to airborne SARS-CoV-2, which causes COVID-19 and other viruses. Many buildings featured in *Good Energy* incorporate operable windows that enable natural ventilation and mechanical ventilation systems that continuously draw in outside air, thereby eliminating the recirculation of inside air.

Novel technologies and approaches that generate renewable energy won't get cut from a project due to budget constraints if they are integrated into projects and serve multiple functions.

Project owners and designers are also increasingly using their net-zero energy projects to educate local communities about the benefits of living with renewable power. In-depth educational websites and in-person or virtual open houses and tours make solutions more real and relatable to K–12 students as well. We especially need students to be optimistic and invested in the future.

Given that numerous US states and cities and the European Union have issued net-zero energy building mandates that will have come into effect in 2020, the pace of innovation in net-zero, energy-positive, and carbon-positive buildings is expected to speed up. While many buildings reduce energy use through practical responsiveness to the site and the environment, technology is also playing an increasingly large role in optimizing building energy systems.

*Good Energy* is, therefore, a snapshot, a moment in time in an innovation continuum. In the coming decade, a whole new set of best practices will likely result from the data collected by increasingly easy-to-use building energy management systems. Strides in decentralized virtual power plant, PV panel, battery, geothermal, and wind turbine technologies are expected to dramatically lower the cost of these technologies, making them accessible to even more people.

# Q&A with Mark Z. Jacobson:
# The Pathways to 100 Percent Renewable Energy

Norway receives 96 percent of its electricity from hydropower. To achieve 100 percent, this Scandinavian country has invested billions to develop multiple onshore and offshore wind farms. Wind power generation capacity reached 2.4 gigawatts in 2019.

**Mark Z. Jacobson has developed roadmaps for** achieving 100 percent renewable energy by 2050 in every US state and 24 global regions, covering 143 countries. His research, which has been published in *Nature, Science, National Geographic, Scientific American*, and numerous other leading journals and publications, underpins the 100 percent renewable energy plans of a number of US states and federal Green New Deal legislation.

Jacobson is a professor of civil and environmental engineering at Stanford University, where he is also the director of the university's Atmosphere/Energy program. He is a senior fellow at the Woods Institute for the Environment and a cofounder of the Solutions Project, 100.org, and the 100 percent Clean, Renewable Energy Movement.

———

## How to Get to 100 Percent

*What is the difference between 100 percent renewable electricity and 100 percent renewable energy?*

Energy includes electricity, transportation energy, building heating and cooling energy, and industrial energy. Electricity is just one component—in fact only 20 percent of all energy. When I say "all energy," I mean end-use energy, which is what people actually use.

*As of January 2020, eleven states and territories in the US have signed laws or executive orders mandating 100 percent renewable electricity by 2045 or 2050. What are the benefits of this approach?*

The key is that there are mandates for a certain percent of renewable electricity by certain dates. This type of policy is what we call a command-and-control policy. They're requiring a certain amount of electricity produced in the state each year to be renewable by a certain date, as opposed to a carbon tax, which raises the price of using fossil fuel–based electricity. A carbon tax doesn't guarantee more electricity will be clean because people might opt to pay the tax and still allow the higher emissions associated with fossil fuels.

Having a mandate (what we call a renewable portfolio standard) has advantages: it requires the elimination of fossil fuels by certain dates. That's a good thing because other types of policies may have that intention but may not actually result in as much reduction in fossil fuels.

*What other incentives, subsidies, mandates, and taxes have been the most effective in accelerating the transition to 100 percent renewable energy?*

Aside from [setting] these renewable portfolio standards, which I think are the most effective way to do it, [we can] mandate standards in other energy sectors. For example, mandate a certain number of vehicles to run on renewable energy by a certain date.

Other methods that have been effective are subsidies and tax credits. For example, there have been solar and wind energy tax credits in the US, so that for every dollar you spend on installing solar or wind, you get 30 cents back as a tax credit. This credit has been very effective at growing the amount of solar and wind and other renewables in the US.

*Approximately 33 percent of global electricity production is now renewable. What is the low-hanging fruit that will enable us to say double that number in a decade?*

The cost of solar photovoltaics (PVs), which can be installed on rooftops, and wind turbines, which can be used in offshore and onshore wind farms, has declined substantially during the past 10 years and continues to decline. As a result, their growth will increase even more in coming years.

We also now have floating offshore wind turbines, so the wind energy infrastructure can be placed even further offshore. Battery-storage costs have come down, and there are now many types of battery storage. Those are all low-hanging fruit for transitioning.

You can transition your own car. The next time you buy a car, go for an electric vehicle (EV) because there are now many carmakers that produce EVs.

You can also transition your own home. It's much cheaper to use electricity, and not gas, in your home, to use heat pumps instead of gas heaters, to use an electric conduction cooktop stove as opposed to a gas stove. You can eliminate gas in your home in favor of renewables and also improve energy efficiency through insulation, LED lights, and low-energy appliances.

In residential, public, and commercial buildings, and with transportation of all types—cars, buses, trucks, even trains—it is possible to go electric and tap into an electric-power sector that is increasingly powered by solar and wind.

***Denmark now gets nearly half of its electricity from wind power. How did they orchestrate this shift over just a couple of decades?***

They have very good offshore- and onshore-wind resources. They were once dependent on imports of energy from other countries, so the shift to

When it started generating power in 2001, the 20-turbine Middlegrunden, which is 3.5 kilometers (2.1 miles) off the coast of Copenhagen, Denmark, was the largest offshore wind facility in the world. Middlegrunden is half owned by Danish utility Hofor, and half-owned by the 10,000 members of a cooperative, making it one of the only offshore community wind farms. The graceful, arcing form was the result of an extensive planning and design process. The wind farm powers approximately 30,000 homes in Copenhagen.

renewables was beneficial because it allowed them to generate much of their own energy.

Denmark incentivized wind energy starting in the 1990s, which resulted in a new wind industry and the growth of many companies that eventually exported their expertise to other countries. The combination of an industrial foothold, a good wind resource, and a demand for homegrown renewable energy resulted in a big wind boon in Denmark.

*Your road maps, which are found via the Solutions Project, recommend various pathways, with different mixes of wind, solar, water, and geothermal energy, to achieve 100 percent renewable energy in US states and 24 global regions covering 143 countries. Are there multiple pathways? How can we predict how renewable energy growth will play out?*

Our research team developed one pathway for each country to get to 100 percent renewables for all energy, but there are multiple renewable pathways. For example, let's say we picked 50 percent wind, 50 percent solar. That's a big oversimplification. We don't actually pick that for any country, but let's say we did. We could've picked 45 percent wind and 55 percent solar or 55 percent wind and 45 percent solar. Those are slightly different pathways, but both possible.

To really determine the best pathway, a more detailed analysis has to be done based on the resources available and the costs of energy and land available because that's how we constrain our pathways. The other important thing is that we have to keep the electric-power grid stable. We performed analyses in which we compared the continuous demand for energy every 30 seconds for three years with the supply of energy from the wind, solar, and geothermal and hydro-electric power, as well as from electricity, heat, cold, and hydrogen storage.

We found we were able to match supply and demand with certain amounts of energy storage in each of the 24 regions of the world covering 143 countries. We tried different mixes and found that we can match power demand and supply and storage with all sorts of mixes of wind and solar in each region. The bottom line is that there are multiple pathways each country and region can follow to become entirely renewable at relatively low cost.

*What countries are furthest ahead in the path to reach 100 percent renewable energy?*

There are 10 countries at or near 100 percent renewables in their electricity sector: Costa Rica, Norway, Iceland, Albania, Paraguay, Uruguay, Tajikistan, Bhutan, Kenya, and Scotland. But electricity is only 20 percent of all end-use energy, so [these countries] really need to transition all other sectors. The countries furthest along with respect to all the sectors are Norway, Iceland, and Tajikistan.

*How will shifting to 100 percent solar, wind, wave, and geothermal reduce overall energy use? How does total electrification reduce energy use?*

If we electrify everything and then create electricity through wind, water, and solar power, we can reduce power demand worldwide by about 57 percent. That is because using heat pumps instead of electric resistance or gas heaters reduces demand for heating on its own by about 75 percent, and using EVs instead of gasoline or diesel cars reduces energy for vehicle transportation by about 75 percent.

Using electric resistance heaters or resistance furnaces for high-temperature industrial processes instead of gas furnaces reduces energy use by a few percent. With these more sustainable furnace

## Megawatts of Wind, Water, and Solar Energy Needed in 2050 (and Percentage Installed at the End of 2018)

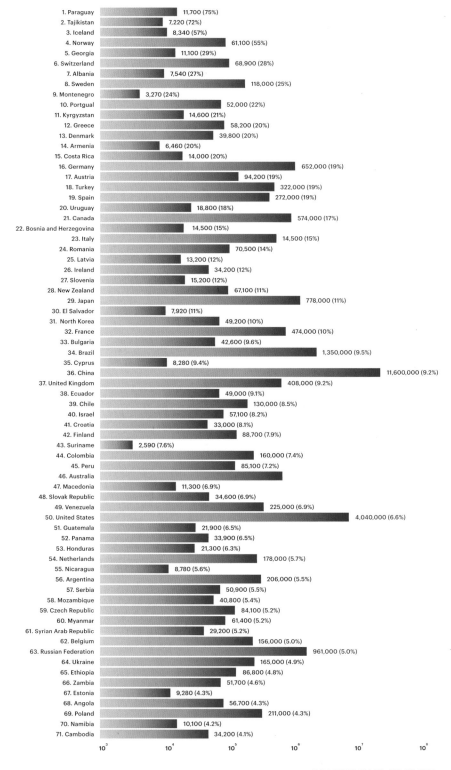

1. Paraguay — 11,700 (75%)
2. Tajikistan — 7,220 (72%)
3. Iceland — 8,340 (57%)
4. Norway — 61,100 (55%)
5. Georgia — 11,100 (29%)
6. Switzerland — 68,900 (28%)
7. Albania — 7,540 (27%)
8. Sweden — 118,000 (25%)
9. Montenegro — 3,270 (24%)
10. Portugal — 52,000 (22%)
11. Kyrgyzstan — 14,600 (21%)
12. Greece — 58,200 (20%)
13. Denmark — 39,800 (20%)
14. Armenia — 6,460 (20%)
15. Costa Rica — 14,000 (20%)
16. Germany — 652,000 (19%)
17. Austria — 94,200 (19%)
18. Turkey — 322,000 (19%)
19. Spain — 272,000 (19%)
20. Uruguay — 18,800 (18%)
21. Canada — 574,000 (17%)
22. Bosnia and Herzegovina — 14,500 (15%)
23. Italy — 14,500 (15%)
24. Romania — 70,500 (14%)
25. Latvia — 13,200 (12%)
26. Ireland — 34,200 (12%)
27. Slovenia — 15,200 (12%)
28. New Zealand — 67,100 (11%)
29. Japan — 778,000 (11%)
30. El Salvador — 7,920 (11%)
31. North Korea — 49,200 (10%)
32. France — 474,000 (10%)
33. Bulgaria — 42,600 (9.6%)
34. Brazil — 1,350,000 (9.5%)
35. Cyprus — 8,280 (9.4%)
36. China — 11,600,000 (9.2%)
37. United Kingdom — 408,000 (9.2%)
38. Ecuador — 49,000 (9.1%)
39. Chile — 130,000 (8.5%)
40. Israel — 57,100 (8.2%)
41. Croatia — 33,000 (8.1%)
42. Finland — 88,700 (7.9%)
43. Suriname — 2,590 (7.6%)
44. Colombia — 160,000 (7.4%)
45. Peru — 85,100 (7.2%)
46. Australia
47. Macedonia — 11,300 (6.9%)
48. Slovak Republic — 34,600 (6.9%)
49. Venezuela — 225,000 (6.9%)
50. United States — 4,040,000 (6.6%)
51. Guatemala — 21,900 (6.5%)
52. Panama — 33,900 (6.5%)
53. Honduras — 21,300 (6.3%)
54. Netherlands — 178,000 (5.7%)
55. Nicaragua — 8,780 (5.6%)
56. Argentina — 206,000 (5.5%)
57. Serbia — 50,900 (5.5%)
58. Mozambique — 40,800 (5.4%)
59. Czech Republic — 84,100 (5.2%)
60. Myanmar — 61,400 (5.2%)
61. Syrian Arab Republic — 29,200 (5.2%)
62. Belgium — 156,000 (5.0%)
63. Russian Federation — 961,000 (5.0%)
64. Ukraine — 165,000 (4.9%)
65. Ethiopia — 86,800 (4.8%)
66. Zambia — 51,700 (4.6%)
67. Estonia — 9,280 (4.3%)
68. Angola — 56,700 (4.3%)
69. Poland — 211,000 (4.3%)
70. Namibia — 10,100 (4.2%)
71. Cambodia — 34,200 (4.1%)

Updated from Mark Z. Jacobson et al., "100 percent Clean and Renewable Wind, Water, and Sunlight All Sector-Energy Roadmaps for 139 Countries in the World," *Joule* 1, 2017, 108–21. Graphic data by Mary A. Cameron.

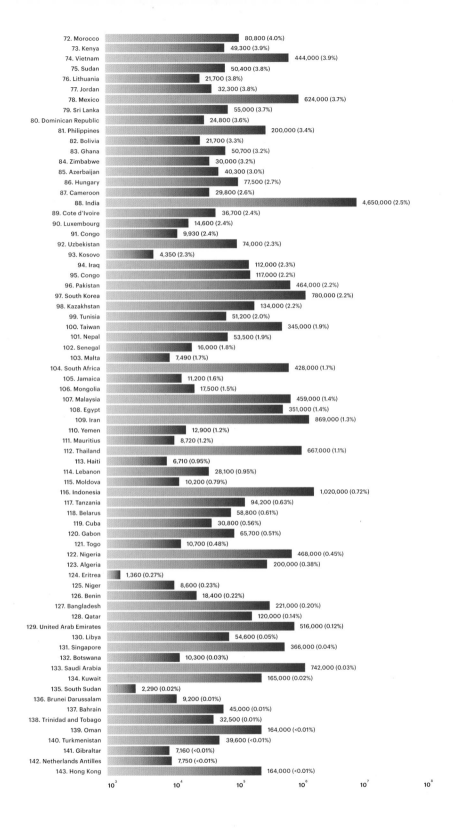

| Rank | Country | Value |
|---|---|---|
| 72. | Morocco | 80,800 (4.0%) |
| 73. | Kenya | 49,300 (3.9%) |
| 74. | Vietnam | 444,000 (3.9%) |
| 75. | Sudan | 50,400 (3.8%) |
| 76. | Lithuania | 21,700 (3.8%) |
| 77. | Jordan | 32,300 (3.8%) |
| 78. | Mexico | 624,000 (3.7%) |
| 79. | Sri Lanka | 55,000 (3.7%) |
| 80. | Dominican Republic | 24,800 (3.6%) |
| 81. | Philippines | 200,000 (3.4%) |
| 82. | Bolivia | 21,700 (3.3%) |
| 83. | Ghana | 50,700 (3.2%) |
| 84. | Zimbabwe | 30,000 (3.2%) |
| 85. | Azerbaijan | 40,300 (3.0%) |
| 86. | Hungary | 77,500 (2.7%) |
| 87. | Cameroon | 29,800 (2.6%) |
| 88. | India | 4,650,000 (2.5%) |
| 89. | Cote d'Ivoire | 36,700 (2.4%) |
| 90. | Luxembourg | 14,600 (2.4%) |
| 91. | Congo | 9,930 (2.4%) |
| 92. | Uzbekistan | 74,000 (2.3%) |
| 93. | Kosovo | 4,350 (2.3%) |
| 94. | Iraq | 112,000 (2.3%) |
| 95. | Congo | 117,000 (2.2%) |
| 96. | Pakistan | 464,000 (2.2%) |
| 97. | South Korea | 780,000 (2.2%) |
| 98. | Kazakhstan | 134,000 (2.2%) |
| 99. | Tunisia | 51,200 (2.0%) |
| 100. | Taiwan | 345,000 (1.9%) |
| 101. | Nepal | 53,500 (1.9%) |
| 102. | Senegal | 16,000 (1.8%) |
| 103. | Malta | 7,490 (1.7%) |
| 104. | South Africa | 428,000 (1.7%) |
| 105. | Jamaica | 11,200 (1.6%) |
| 106. | Mongolia | 17,500 (1.5%) |
| 107. | Malaysia | 459,000 (1.4%) |
| 108. | Egypt | 351,000 (1.4%) |
| 109. | Iran | 869,000 (1.3%) |
| 110. | Yemen | 12,900 (1.2%) |
| 111. | Mauritius | 8,720 (1.2%) |
| 112. | Thailand | 667,000 (1.1%) |
| 113. | Haiti | 6,710 (0.95%) |
| 114. | Lebanon | 28,100 (0.95%) |
| 115. | Moldova | 10,200 (0.79%) |
| 116. | Indonesia | 1,020,000 (0.72%) |
| 117. | Tanzania | 94,200 (0.63%) |
| 118. | Belarus | 58,800 (0.61%) |
| 119. | Cuba | 30,800 (0.56%) |
| 120. | Gabon | 65,700 (0.51%) |
| 121. | Togo | 10,700 (0.48%) |
| 122. | Nigeria | 468,000 (0.45%) |
| 123. | Algeria | 200,000 (0.38%) |
| 124. | Eritrea | 1,360 (0.27%) |
| 125. | Niger | 8,600 (0.23%) |
| 126. | Benin | 18,400 (0.22%) |
| 127. | Bangladesh | 221,000 (0.20%) |
| 128. | Qatar | 120,000 (0.14%) |
| 129. | United Arab Emirates | 516,000 (0.12%) |
| 130. | Libya | 54,600 (0.05%) |
| 131. | Singapore | 366,000 (0.04%) |
| 132. | Botswana | 10,300 (0.03%) |
| 133. | Saudi Arabia | 742,000 (0.03%) |
| 134. | Kuwait | 165,000 (0.02%) |
| 135. | South Sudan | 2,290 (0.02%) |
| 136. | Brunei Darussalam | 9,200 (0.01%) |
| 137. | Bahrain | 45,000 (0.01%) |
| 138. | Trinidad and Tobago | 32,500 (0.01%) |
| 139. | Oman | 164,000 (<0.01%) |
| 140. | Turkmenistan | 39,600 (<0.01%) |
| 141. | Gibraltar | 7,160 (<0.01%) |
| 142. | Netherlands Antilles | 7,750 (<0.01%) |
| 143. | Hong Kong | 164,000 (<0.01%) |

$10^3$  $10^4$  $10^5$  $10^6$  $10^7$  $10^8$

# 100% EARTH

A vision for the transition to 100% wind, water & solar energy.

 Residential rooftop solar
**5.4%**

 Commercial & government rooftop solar
**9.9%**

 Solar plants
**26.5%**

 Wave devices
**.3%**

 Concentrating solar plants
**2.4%**

 Geothermal
**.7%**

 Onshore wind
**38.2%**

 Hydroelectric
**5%**

 Offshore wind
**11.5%**

 Tidal Turbines
**.1%**

## 2050
**PROJECTED ENERGY MIX**

### 40-Year Jobs Created
Number of jobs where a person is employed for 40 consecutive years

Construction jobs: **24,389,000**

Operation jobs: **30,151,000**

## Reducing Energy Demand

Improving energy efficiency and powering the grid with electricity from the wind, water, and sun positively reduces the overall energy demand.

**Current demand**

**Wind, water, solar**

**-57%**

THE**SOLUTIONS**PROJECT

www.thesolutionsproject.org
Data from Stanford University

options, we also no longer mine fossil fuels or uranium, so we can eliminate about 12 percent of all energy use for mining worldwide, transporting, and refining fossil fuels and uranium. Solar comes right to the panel; wind comes right to the turbine.

When you add all this up and also account for additional end-use energy-efficiency improvements, we can reduce energy-consumption demand by about 57 percent average over all energy sectors. Even if your cost per unit of energy is similar between fossil fuels and wind, wood, or solar, your cost is actually 57 percent lower because you're using 57 percent less energy. But we also find that the cost per unit energy is about 10 percent lower. The overall cost savings is about 60 percent by going to clean renewable energy.

### In which areas have you seen the most progress during the past decade?

There's been progress in laws being passed and then progress in actual implementation. In terms of laws being passed, the United States has actually been pretty successful.

At the state level, there are now 11 states and territories that have either laws or executive orders to go to 100 percent renewables in the electricity sector. At the local level, there are 142 or more cities and towns that have laws to [transition] to 100 percent renewables. Internationally, there are over 220 international companies that have committed to 100 percent renewables. In terms of policies, I'm really pleased with the progress.

In terms of implementation, many countries have gone much further than they were a decade ago. But it's not only how much further they've gone, it's that there are now a lot more countries committed to going far. There are now 61 countries that have committed to 100 percent renewable electric power. And, as I mentioned, there are 10 that have reached nearly 100 percent renewable in the electricity sector.

The public, based on public-opinion polling, wants to transition. The costs have come down for solar, wind, batteries, and electric cars. I can't possibly have asked for a better convergence of laws, reduced costs, improvements in technology, and public willpower to transition. I'm optimistic that a transition can occur on a large scale because of all these good things that have happened.

———

**Health Benefits of Renewable Energy**

*According to the World Health Organization, there are some 7 million premature deaths annually that result from stroke, heart disease, chronic obstructive pulmonary disease, lung cancer, and acute respiratory infections. Air pollution also increases the danger of asthma, particularly for vulnerable populations in cities. What are the health costs of bad air worldwide? How will clean, renewable energy help solve this problem?*

Yes, 7 million people die every year from air pollution, and hundreds of millions more are made ill. If the world doesn't move to 100 percent renewable energy, the worldwide cost of this would be on the order of $30 trillion per year in 2050, which would be equal to 9.29 percent of global GDP. It's enormous. These costs can be avoided by eliminating air pollution.

Our plan not only eliminates the chemicals that affect the global climate but also the chemicals that affect people's health, which results in a huge social-cost saving in addition to an energy-cost savings.

Our plan will reduce energy costs by 60 percent, but it reduces total social costs (energy costs plus health costs plus climate costs) by about 90 percent compared to fossil fuels. It's an enormous cost savings.

*Fossil fuel–powered cars generate air particulate matter—black carbon—which is a major contributor to air pollution. In developing countries, low-quality fuels with high pollutant loads exacerbate the problem. China and other countries are incentivizing the shift to cleaner EVs in order to improve air quality. Can you identify the specific health costs of fossil fuel–powered vehicles? How can EVs help solve the problem?*

Currently, energy generation causes about 90 to 95 percent of air pollution. Vehicle transportation is on the order of 27 percent of all energy consumption. Roughly then, we're talking about [the fact that] 27 percent of air-pollution deaths are from transportation. If we clean up transportation worldwide, we can reduce about 27 percent of those deaths.

———

### Planning and Designing Renewable Energy

*You have estimated that as many as 3.08 million wind turbines, each generating 5 megawatts, could be needed globally. You have found this is doable given an estimated 70 million cars are produced each year, which means that there's more than enough steel. How else can land dedicated to the generation of wind power be used?*

Wind is unique. It doesn't actually require much land—or what we call a footprint—because a turbine is a pole stuck in the ground. Farmers love to have wind turbines on their property because they can get additional revenue without using up much land. Farmers can grow crops in between wind turbines and get royalties from power production.

Land between turbines can be used for farming and also for ranching, for grazing, or as green open space. With wind turbines, there can be multipurpose uses of land, which is not the case with fossil fuels.

We can also put solar panels between wind turbines. Or wind turbines can be put in the ocean, where they're not taking up any land already in use.

*You have found that many more renewable power plants would also be needed in order to reach 100 percent renewable energy: an estimated 130,000 concentrated solar plants, each generating 100 megawatts, and 268,000 PV solar plants, each generating 50 megawatts. Given the benefits of multipurpose infrastructure, how can solar power plants be conjoined with other infrastructure to make them more efficient?*

Solar is already being integrated into commercial, governmental, and residential buildings in many ways, but it can also be integrated with water systems. If you have water underneath solar panels, the water helps keep the solar panels cool. Cooler solar panels function far more efficiently than hot ones. Some of the heat absorbed by the water can also provide a source of hot water in a building.

You can also combine solar-power generation with growing food. For example, in remote communities in Alaska, where it gets really cold and most food must be imported, people can grow food in a greenhouse powered by solar or wind. Greenhouses powered by renewables can generate electricity that can produce ultraviolet light or more visible light to grow plants.

Even at high latitudes, you can produce a lot of energy from PV panels by tracking the sun. In fact, most people don't realize this, but the spot on the Earth, on annual average, with the most solar radiation that could hit a panel if you tracked the sun is the South Pole. The South Pole is elevated, and the higher up you go, the stronger

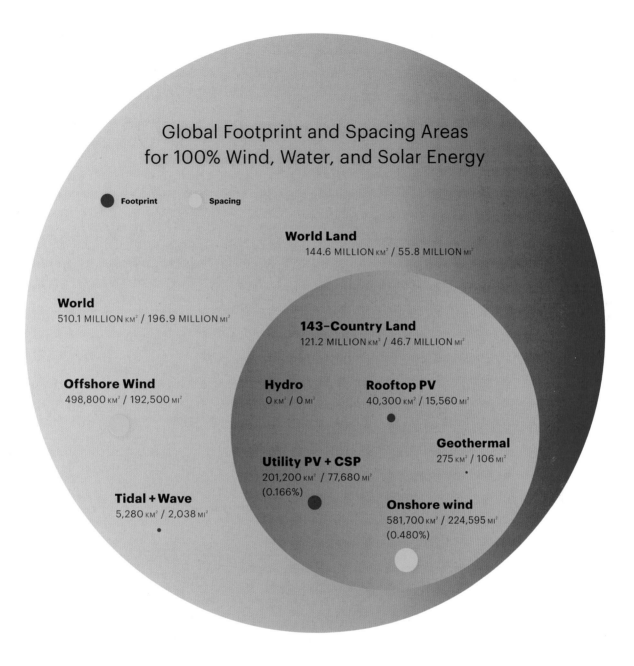

Global Footprint and Spacing Areas
for 100% Wind, Water, and Solar Energy

● Footprint    ○ Spacing

**World Land**
144.6 MILLION KM² / 55.8 MILLION MI²

**World**
510.1 MILLION KM² / 196.9 MILLION MI²

**143–Country Land**
121.2 MILLION KM² / 46.7 MILLION MI²

**Offshore Wind**
498,800 KM² / 192,500 MI²

**Hydro**
0 KM² / 0 MI²

**Rooftop PV**
40,300 KM² / 15,560 MI²

**Geothermal**
275 KM² / 106 MI²

**Utility PV + CSP**
201,200 KM² / 77,680 MI²
(0.166%)

**Tidal + Wave**
5,280 KM² / 2,038 MI²

**Onshore wind**
581,700 KM² / 224,595 MI²
(0.480%)

Updated from Mark Z. Jacobson et al., "100 percent Clean
and Renewable Wind, Water, and Sunlight All Sector-Energy
Roadmaps for 139 Countries in the World," *Joule* 1, 2017,
108–21. Graphic data by Mary A. Cameron.

the radiation is. So even in cold climates, if solar panels are angled to track the sun, communities can get a reasonable amount of sunlight. There are multiple ways to combine food, energy, and water systems with renewables at the center of the system producing energy.

*The planning and design communities are increasingly focused on ensuring local energy resilience to climate impacts, such as floods, wildfires, and rising sea levels. This means more neighborhood- or district-scale power plants that are not only resilient to these impacts but also more visible and more connected to a community's sense of safety and identity, perhaps more so than some distant utility-sized renewable power plant. What is the case for community energy?*

There are two types of community energy. There's what we call a microgrid, which is an isolated grid in which all of the community's energy is produced locally by solar, wind, geothermal, and hydroelectric power. That's pretty common on islands.

In fact, Puerto Rico, which recently had its whole energy and transmission system destroyed, is rebuilding it as 100 percent renewable energy infrastructure, breaking the island into six to ten microgrids. Each microgrid can be run on its own but will also be connected to the other ones for normal operation. If one part goes down, the others are resilient and can maintain themselves. That's an ideal situation for isolated communities.

There's also what we call regular distributed energy, which depends on a conventional energy grid but in which many individual homes and governmental and commercial buildings produce their own energy through rooftop solar. If the power does go out, they can still use their own electricity to keep their lights on. In my house, I have solar on the roof and batteries in the garage, so if the utility grid goes down, my batteries kick

in and produce electricity at night. My solar still works and produces electricity for the batteries through the day, so they'll run days on end without a problem. This is distributed energy, as opposed to the centralized energy of these big power plants that distribute energy to everybody.

The fact is that we don't have enough rooftops to provide all the electricity we need for all of our purposes. Our analysis shows that, for the US, we propose that 11 percent of all energy will be obtained from rooftop PVs on homes and 14.6 percent from PVs on commercial and government buildings. Worldwide, the numbers are 11.1 percent and 13.8 percent, respectively, so we also need large-scale solar and wind farms.

In terms of wind, it's much more efficient to have a wind farm with tall turbines than it is to have short wind turbines because wind gets faster with height from the ground. In wind farms, each turbine is its own power plant and independent. If one turbine goes down, all the other ones are still running. That's different than a centralized power plant in which if a turbine goes down, most of the plant's power is shut off.

———

**Transmission and Storage**

*In the seventies and eighties, Buckminster Fuller called for a global interconnected energy grid that would transmit renewable energy from continent to continent, from rural areas to population centers—a true internet of energy. Does this vision still have value?*

In theory, it's a great idea, but in practice you don't need to transmit all the energy. You can produce and store a lot of it locally.

Two extremes are 100 percent transmission or 100 percent storage. One extreme is a system in which local wind and solar power plants and rooftop PV panels produce all the energy

Solar-panel technicians install PV panels on the roof of a barn at Grange farm, near Balcombe, United Kingdom. The installation is a part of the REPOWERBalcombe initiative, which aims to meet 100 percent of Balcomb's energy needs through community-owned locally generated renewable energy.

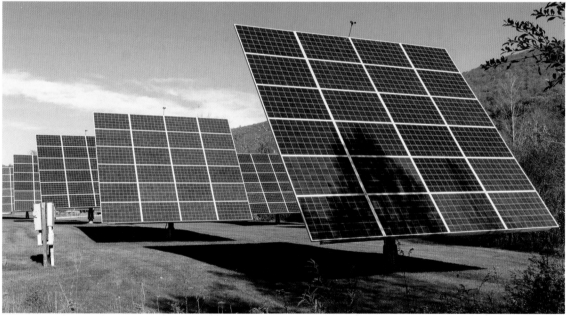

Solar panels in Manchester, Vermont, rotate to track the sun, improving their ability to generate electricity by 25 to 35 percent.

Electricity-transmission lines, like the ones seen here in California, are expensive and time-consuming to plan and develop. Renewable energy systems should leverage existing networks of transmission lines wherever possible.

a community needs, transmit it to homes and buildings locally, and then store the rest as extra electricity. Another extreme is in which there are a few places that produce all of the electricity, and a huge transmission system transmits the electricity everywhere. There is no need for storage because somewhere in the world, electricity is produced from wind or solar at any given second and transmitted to where it is needed. We really don't need a complete global energy grid at all. But we do need a mix of transmission and storage.

It's important to favor storage more than transmission because transmission lines are very difficult to site. They are not technically difficult to install. The upfront costs are expensive, but transmission lines last a long time and can pay for themselves over time. It's just very difficult to get agreement with property owners to put

a lot of transmission lines everywhere. Batteries for storage can be placed almost anywhere, and people will not complain.

*Does the current transmission infrastructure pose an obstacle in the shift to renewable energy sources?*

No, in fact, the existing transmission network works perfectly well whether the energy source is coal, nuclear, solar, or wind. We want to keep the existing transmission infrastructure to the extent we can and grow it where it's needed.

*In recent research, you have analyzed how regional grids can be optimized to handle intermittency issues presented by wind and solar. Wind farms generate power when the wind blows, solar when the sun is bright. Do these sources have to be paired with more consistent energy sources to ensure grid stability? Or is storage the solution?*

There is not only electricity storage but also heat, cold, and hydrogen storage. The future system will be different from the one we have today, which focuses on electricity storage, because once we electrify building heating and cooling, vehicles, and industry, we will not only have more storage options but also more options for what we call demand response.

The goal is to meet instantaneous demand for energy, which can be met in two ways. You can either meet it with electricity, heat or cold, or whatever type of energy you need. Or you can reduce demand.

If you can give someone an incentive not to use electricity for the next 10 minutes, that means you can shift electricity use to a different time of the day. That's called demand response—you incentivize people to not use electricity at a certain time of day. One way to do that is to have different rates of electricity for different times of the day. Let's say you have an EV. You don't need

to plug a wind turbine into the car directly because the EV has a battery. You can charge that vehicle pretty much any time, day or night.

If you have an excess supply of wind and a low demand for energy late at night, why not give people incentives to charge their cars at night? To do that, you need to have a lower electricity price at night and a higher one during the day. This gives people an incentive to charge the vehicle during the night when you have excess electricity. This is what I do in my neighborhood in California where we have really low nighttime rates and really high daytime rates. This incentive shifts the time of energy use.

Communities can also use demand response with water heating. You don't need to heat the water at any specific time. You can heat it up pretty much anytime day or night. Water heating for some industrial processes can also take advantage of demand response. There are also lots of options for low-cost heat, cold, and hydrogen storage.

Electricity storage is more expensive, but it's coming down in cost. By combining storage with demand response, we can match power demand with supply everywhere in the world just using renewable energy.

EVs can be charged at night when energy demand and prices are lower. Utilities and EV-charger companies can also further incentivize nighttime charging by providing financial or other benefits or rewards. Given the intermittency of wind and solar energy generation, energy-management technologies and energy-storage systems will be needed to manage daily fluctuations in energy demand.

## Potential Risks

*With climate change, we have seen weather patterns change, adding to future uncertainty. Does a fully solar-, wind-, water-, and geothermal-powered electricity grid increase our risks? Imagine a future California or Australia powered entirely by wind and solar. Would expanding wildfires reduce the ability of rooftop PV panels or solar farms to generate electricity?*

Solar power is distributed, so at any given time, many places have little or no smoke and ash.

If there are centralized power plants and one or two of those burn down because they're in the path of a fire, then you're permanently losing a large amount of power when you have a forest fire. There's greater risk when you have centralized power plants.

In that respect, distributed solar is less risky. Rooftop PV panels will take both direct sunlight and scattered light, which is light that bounces off of little particles in the air. Even with forest fire smoke, there's still scattered light. The bigger issue is when there is cloud coverage.

*One of your studies found that a global shift to 100 percent renewable would yield 28.6 million more jobs globally than would be lost due to the phasing out of fossil fuel–related industries. What is the best way to address the social disruption this may cause?*

The transition is occurring. I wouldn't say slowly, but not likely all tomorrow. We're trying to get to 80 percent renewable energy by 2030 and 100 percent by 2050.

There will be job losses in some industries. People will have to be retrained to go into other industries. But there will be more job gains than losses, so there will be a net benefit. Unfortunately, this will cause some families to experience a temporary disruption.

In the end, the transition will benefit more people than it doesn't. It's only positive to have such a transition. We've had many transitions in the past. In the lead-up to World War II, there was a transition of jobs, industry, and manufacturing. It has happened before and can happen again.

*Is there a renewable energy jobs-retraining program that has worked? Have we been able to successfully transition people working in a coal mine to work with wind turbines?*

The best example I can give is with offshore oil drilling. A lot of offshore workers in the oil business go into building offshore wind turbines and farms because the offshore oil industry is very similar to the offshore wind industry. Both of these platforms are floating devices, so there are similar technologies.

Coal miners can go into installing solar, which doesn't require a huge amount of training. There are more people employed in the solar industry now than in the oil and gas industry combined in the United States. They are coming from some-where—whether from coal or another type of job.

**Author's Note:** While we didn't get to the topic in the interview, Jacobson has outlined another potential barrier to scaling up wind and solar power and the use of EVs worldwide: materials used in these technologies could become "scarce or subject to price manipulation." These include rare-earth metals, for example: neodymium used in magnets in wind-turbine gearboxes; lithium for lithium-ion batteries used in EVs; silver, tellurium, and indium used in solar cells; and platinum, which can be used in fuel cells.

However, Jacobson believes this barrier isn't insurmountable. New technologies and materials and the recycling of materials provide solutions.

With the growth of gearless wind turbines, the future cost and availability of neodymium may become moot. There are other materials that can be used in magnets as well.

More than half of the world's lithium supply exists in Chile and Bolivia. With increased demand for lithium-ion batteries, prices could significantly increase. Engineering EV batteries that can be recycled in an affordable way would help expand the availability of lithium and avoid that bottleneck. Furthermore, in *Scientific American*, Jacobson contends that the long-term use of silver and platinum also depends on greater recycling of these materials.

As the renewable energy transition accelerates, demand for rare-earth metals, and other key materials used in these technologies, is expected to significantly increase, creating new pressure to create dependable local sources and open up new recycling industries. Given that the extraction of many of these materials results in high environmental and public health costs, recycling is the most sustainable way forward. Local recycling industries for PV panels, batteries, and other materials could also lead to thousands of new green jobs.

According to the US Department of Energy, a robust US offshore wind energy industry could create 46,000 jobs. Currently, in the US, annual salaries for offshore wind technicians range from $37,000 to $71,000. The American Wind Energy Association states that onshore wind supports some 114,000 jobs.

Chapter One

# POWER HOMES

## Power Homes

—

### Houses, Apartment Complexes, and Residential Communities

Homes of any size and for any income level can be designed to meet their own energy needs. A key foundation of this transformation—the photovoltaic (PV) panel—is quickly becoming a standard feature on roofs around the world. Once this increasingly low-cost technology is in place, every residence can be sophisticated enough to meet its own energy demand and supply 24-7 through batteries and energy-management systems.

In the near future, decentralized virtual power plants made of networked rooftop PV panels and batteries are expected to manage an increased share of energy supply and demand. They may even supplant many centralized power plants. The benefits of participatory, decentralized energy infrastructure are improved resilience to climate and other weather shocks, increased efficiency, reduced energy costs, and even profits.

Yet the rooftop PV—or any other form of residential energy generation—is really just one component in making a single-family house, apartment complex, or residential community net-zero energy or energy-positive. All homes need to fully electrify, eliminating the use of coal, oil, and gas in boilers, furnaces, and stoves, which not only pollute but also contribute to unhealthy indoor air. Buildings need to incorporate low-energy appliances, insulation, and energy-efficient windows.

Finally and perhaps most important, passive house techniques should be used to achieve deep energy savings from heating, cooling, and ventilation. The term "passive house" refers to a set of techniques that essentially turn a house or apartment building into an airtight ship that doesn't leak heat in the winter or require much cooling in the summer. These homes are designed with the seasonal path of the sun in mind, maximizing solar heat gain in the winter and reducing it in the summer. They can also be designed around the daily movements of the sun, inviting in light at certain times and blocking it when temperatures are warmest in the afternoon. Passive houses and apartment buildings can reduce energy use by up to 90 percent over conventional building practices and provide much healthier indoor air. These projects don't have to cost more either.

With the global population expected to grow to nearly 11.2 billion people by 2100, the need for new sustainable-housing models is critical. The world currently has an estimated 1.6 billion households, and an estimated 2 billion new homes will be needed by 2100. To protect our remaining ecosystems and biological diversity, there needs to be more compact infill development in urban and suburban centers. Development outside these areas should be strictly reserved for regenerative projects that support ecological preservation and restoration.

If we want to keep warming below 1.5 degrees Celsius (2.7 degrees Fahrenheit), as outlined in the Paris Climate Accord, and thereby limit the dangerous impacts of climate change, we need to retrofit existing homes to be net-zero energy by 2050 and build all new homes to meet the new net-zero energy standard by 2030. For new buildings, prefabrication, which increases efficiency in construction, often makes a great deal of sense.

In developed countries, far less than 1 percent of homes are built to the net-zero energy standard.

However, that will soon dramatically change. The State of California and the European Commission have mandated net-zero energy homes moving forward, which is expected to add hundreds of thousands of these new and retrofitted homes in coming years. Furthermore, as of June 2020, 28 major cities, including New York City and Washington, DC, in the US, Medellín in Colombia, and Cape Town and Johannesburg in South Africa, representing more than 125 million people, have committed to achieving net-zero energy building operations by 2050. Still, many more governments at all levels need to join the effort and ratchet up their commitments.

Power Homes features net-zero energy and energy-positive houses, apartment complexes, and residential communities around the world that fit a variety of income levels. In the middle-income range, there are inventive projects such as SMA x ECO TOWN Harumidai in Sakai City, Japan, a fully energy-positive community that turns energy reduction into a game in which residents earn points to be redeemed for free rides in community electric vehicles (EVs). The Power of 10 in Örebro, Sweden, shows that the standard townhouse found in any community can be designed to be net-zero in energy use, gorgeous, and built out of prefabricated modules in an efficient manner.

The Zero Carbon House in Birmingham, United Kingdom, is one of the best examples of how to retrofit an older house to become energy-positive, and save most of the embodied carbon stored in original materials. Trent Basin, also in the UK, shows how communities can become a virtual power plant, using rooftop PVs and powerful batteries to manage energy demand, save money, and support grid resilience.

At the luxury end, the Connecticut Residence, an ecologically responsible, net-zero energy single-family house, combines rooftop PV and passive house techniques with a geothermal system that reduces energy use for heating and cooling and supports both human and ecological health. And at a larger scale, the Sustainable City, a nearly net-zero energy international community in the United Arab Emirates, is designed to improve the health and well-being of some three thousand expats and local residents.

At the lower income level, Belfield Townhomes in Philadelphia, Pennsylvania, demonstrates that net-zero energy passive houses can be built fast and at a very low price per square foot. M-KOPA Solar in East Africa, which *MIT Technology Review* named one of the 50 smartest companies in the world, demonstrates how to give the billions of people who don't have access to the energy grid the experience of light, TV, radio, and cell-phone charging at an affordable rate while also significantly improving indoor air quality.

Many residential communities in Power Homes also highlight the important health |benefits of integrating green open space into living environments as well. While communities manage COVID-19 along with the long-term health epidemics of stress and obesity, spaces where residents can safely walk and bike, breathe fresh air, and experience nature reduce stress and improve mental and physical health and well-being.

# UC Davis West Village
Davis, California, United States

**At 224 acres (90 hectares), the West** Village at University of California, Davis, is one of the largest planned sustainable communities in the US. The university's ambitious vision— to become a laboratory for how to live with renewable energy—was conceived in 2003. It was realized a decade later through a public-private partnership with the West Village Community Partnership, a joint venture between two developers: Carmel Partners and Urban Villages. Today, West Village produces nearly 90 percent of its own energy, proving the benefit of a holistic approach to reducing energy that also improves community health.

In partnership with the university, the developers assembled a multidisciplinary team, including UC Davis Energy and Efficiency Institute, Davis Energy Group, and Chevron Energy Partners; architects, urban planners, and designers at Moore Ruble Yudell, Mogavero Architects, Studio E Architects, and MVE Architects; and open space and landscape planners and designers at SWA Group. The goal was to create a comprehensive master plan for an environmentally responsive, walkable, bikeable, healthy community to be built in phases.

UC Davis and the developers sought to incorporate innovative energy-efficiency strategies and some combination of wind, solar, or geothermal energy sources without sacrificing design quality or adding costs for the developers or community members. The university didn't mandate net-zero energy, but that goal soon became a driver of the planning and design team.

Through an in-depth site analysis based in energy modeling by Davis Energy Group and SunPower, the planning and design team optimized the configuration of apartment buildings and open spaces for rooftop solar power generation and building-energy efficiency. The southern orientation of the roofs of the mixed-use buildings maximizes renewable-energy generation through PV panels. Community-wide energy use was reduced by designing streets and open spaces to maximize afternoon breezes coming from the southwest and planting hundreds of trees to shade and cool buildings and community spaces. These same strategies also create a healthy, comfortable environment for community residents and the public.

In 2013, the $280 million first phase, covering 130 acres, opened with a network of publicly accessible green recreation spaces, including a central Village Square. There are 663 apartments that provide housing for two thousand faculty, staff, and students; 42,500 square feet (3,950 square meters) of office and commercial space; the Sacramento City College Davis Center, a community college; and a consolidated home for the campus's renewable energy research centers. An additional phase now in development will add 1,250 student-housing units for three thousands students.

West Village's apartment buildings, mixed-use buildings, and even parking-lot canopies are covered in rooftop PV panels with a 4-megawatt capacity. Buildings also benefit from passive house approaches that significantly reduce energy use.

SWA Group, which led planning, design, and development phases of the landscape architecture, built on the existing bicycling culture of the campus to create a bicycle-first transportation system that further reduces greenhouse gas emissions from transportation and improves residents' health. Studies have shown that bicycling to work, instead of driving, significantly reduces the risk of cardiovascular disease, cancer, and premature death from other causes.

West Villages makes bicycling easy. Some five miles of trails connect cyclists to the rest of the campus and university bus stops. Bicycle parking was integrated into the building courtyards and public spaces, whereas vehicle parking is located under central structures farther away from buildings. No resident is more than a quarter of a mile from a campus bus line.

West Village shows what is possible through a sustainable community-design approach. But the developers argue there are also some important lessons learned. According to Nolan Zail, former senior vice president of development for Carmel Partners and one of the executives on the project, there are a few reasons why the development fell just shy of its very ambitious goal of net-zero energy use: "The initial energy-use models were very limited on data, specifically energy use for student housing. Energy use has been higher than anticipated, and there were more students than anticipated. Also, system performance changed over time—some of the technologies initially used did not perform as anticipated." He added that "regulatory complexities in California made it challenging to establish business models and user incentives to reduce energy consumption."

Despite the challenges, West Village shows the great merit of designing communities, buildings, landscape, and transportation as one system to reduce energy use and improve health and well-being.

OPPOSITE TOP **Apartment buildings and parking lot canopies alike are covered in PV panels. Given that street parking reduces density and easy access to cars can reduce the incentive to walk or bike, the development, planning, and design team moved parking into centralized areas.**

OPPOSITE BOTTOM **The landscape design team sited bicycle parking close to residences, making it very easy to hop on a bike and go. Trees alongside the buildings and above the bicycle parking spaces keep the buildings cooler and reduce energy use and also create a more livable, healthy environment.**

Tapping into the existing biking culture at UC Davis, SWA Group proposed a bicycle-centric transportation system for West Village, with 5 miles (8 kilometers) of trails set within green spaces that double as stormwater management systems. Privileging biking helps reduce greenhouse gas emissions resulting from transportation.

# Sweetwater Spectrum
Sonoma, California, United States

**Roughly 1 percent of the world's** population, or 70 million people, are on the autism spectrum. According to the Centers for Disease Control and Prevention (CDC), 1 in 59 children in the US are identified as being on the spectrum.

At an Environmental Design Research Association conference a few years ago, Sherry Ahrentzen, a professor of housing studies at the University of Florida and a coauthor of the book *At Home with Autism: Designing Housing for the Spectrum*, explained that there is no one size fits all approach to caring for people with autism: "If you know one person with autism, you really know just one person with autism."

Ahrentzen explained that people with autism have a "blend of cognitive strengths and weaknesses." In general, they are capable of "detailed thinking, expansive long-term thinking, and examining complex patterns." But they may also have problems with "understanding social nuances, filtering stimuli, and planning daily living." People with autism can be overwhelmed by visual stimulation, sound, lighting, and odors.

In the coming decade, an estimated 500,000 American children with autism will reach adulthood, and many will need residential environments that are calming and supportive. About 80,000 adults with autism are already on waiting lists for placements in appropriate housing, some with waits as long as a decade.

In 2009, a group of families with children with autism collaborated with civic leaders and professionals to create a nonprofit organization called Sweetwater Spectrum. Their vision was to plan and design a new kind of community that helps adults with autism live a "life with purpose."

Four years later, Sweetwater Spectrum opened on 2.8 acres (1.1 hectares) of infill property a few blocks from the town square of Sonoma, California. Leveraging research into both autism and sustainable design, they created a pilot community the group hopes will become a national model for supportive housing for adults with autism.

The 16 residents of Sweetwater Spectrum, who are aged 22 to 38, come and go as they please. Former interim executive director Carol Patterson told the *Press Democrat*: "Some are high functioning to not so high. Some require 24-hour help." Residents pay rent and activities fees, but there are also subsidies to ensure a diverse community. As of 2016, Sweetwater Spectrum has raised $8.2 million from more than two hundred donors to pay for the $10.4 million project and maintain operations.

The net-zero energy community, designed by Leddy Maytum Stacy Architects (LMSA) and Roche + Roche Landscape Architecture, has four houses, each with four bedrooms, a shared kitchen, a living room, and a terrace. The community also offers a center with a library, gym, and spaces for art and music; a therapeutic swimming pool and two hot tubs; and a 1.2-acre (0.5-hectare) organic vegetable garden and orchard that also has a greenhouse and chicken coop. All of these elements are connected through easy-to-understand paths, both inside the buildings and outside, that enable residents to better control how they experience the environment.

According to Roche + Roche: "The progression of spaces from private room, to shared house, to the Sweetwater campus, to the greater Sonoma community is carefully designed to allow residents the ability to advance or retreat as needed. Spaces are designed to be simple and predictable, with transitions from one space to another left open to allow previewing of the next space."

The four houses and community center were designed to achieve

OPPOSITE **At Sweetwater Spectrum, 16 residents with autism live in a community purposefully designed to help them thrive. The four net-zero houses and community center were designed to achieve net-zero energy use and minimize visual stimulation, ambient sound, lighting, and odors.**

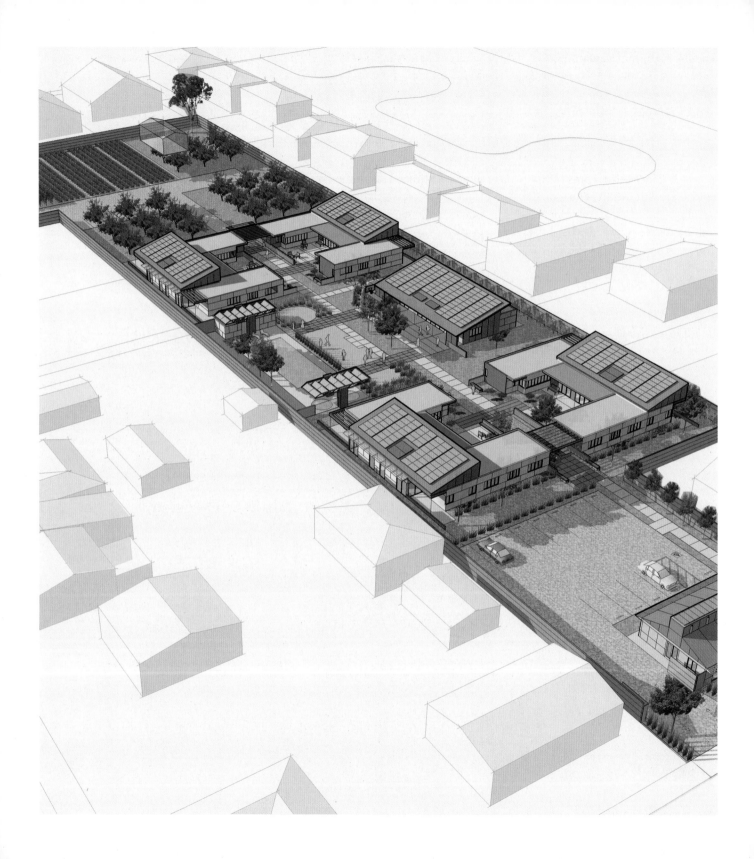

net-zero energy use and minimize visual stimulation, ambient sound, lighting, and odors. LMSA states that extra care was taken to select building materials and systems that promote healthy indoor air, acoustical control, and comfortable temperatures. For example, "since ceiling fans can be a negative stimulus to people on the autism spectrum, a radiant slab heating and cooling system was used with a low-velocity ventilation system."

The houses and community center are oriented not only to maximize daylight and natural ventilation, which helps create a serene environment, but also to optimize renewable energy production via rooftop PV solar panels. To improve energy efficiency, buildings incorporated high levels of insulation and high-performance windows that also help reduce noise and glare and "cool" roofs and overhangs, trellises, and operable exterior sunshades that also keep indoor spaces comfortable.

Residences include high efficiency air-to-water heat pumps, energy-efficient lighting, Energy Star appliances, and induction cooktops, which all reduce energy use. LMSA found these strategies resulted in energy performance 30 percent better than California's Title 24 energy requirements.

OPPOSITE **The site plan for Sweetwater Spectrum shows how rooftop PV solar panels are angled south to maximize access to sunlight and therefore energy production. The plan also shows the clear paths that enable residents to preview spaces.**

RIGHT **In the background is the highly energy-efficient community center and, to the right, one of the four residential houses both powered by rooftop PV solar panels. In the foreground is Sweetwater Spectrum's pool, which is used for water therapy. Many people with autism are drawn to water, and swimming therapy has been shown to effectively build social, emotional, and cognitive skills and support self-confidence.**

According to Roche + Roche Landscape Architecture, "Water features are absent, and shade structures are either solid or of simple design to eliminate distracting refraction and shade/light patterns. The plant pallet is mostly 'quiet,' using subtle and soothing variations of foliage color and form, and avoiding profusions of brightly colored blooms." A well provides water for irrigation systems in the community landscape, including the organic farm and orchards. Drought-tolerant plants minimize the need to irrigate. Permeable pavers and bioswales absorb stormwater.

# Connecticut Residence
Connecticut, United States

The cypress wood-clad house, which
is oriented to the south, surrounds a
constructed lake.

**A couple who served on the board of** the National Audubon Society, which aims to conserve land and protect birds and their habitat, wanted to build a house that reflected their deep environmental values. The result is a net-zero energy house featuring geothermal and solar energy systems that supports and enhances nature.

They purchased 10 acres (4 hectares) of land that bisects a 750-acre (303-hectare) nature preserve and 40-acre (16-hectare) conservation area near Long Island Sound in Connecticut. Half of the site is in a conservation easement with a land trust, meaning it is protected from development. On the other half, the homeowners wanted to break down barriers between inside and outside, between the house and the surrounding ecosystem.

The 8,000-square-foot (743-square-meter) Connecticut Residence, designed by James Cutler and a team of architects at Cutler Anderson, along with pond designer Anthony Archer-Wills and landscape architect Diane Devore, surrounds a pond that was dug and filled with water flowing from a creek at the north end of the site and is now replenished by runoff from the main building's roof. The pond is the centerpiece of the house's layout, attracting insects, frogs, fish, and birds, including blue herons. From the floor-to-ceiling "infinity windows" throughout the house's bedrooms, living spaces, and hallways, the drama of the surrounding ecology is ever present.

The homeowners give back to nature through the construction of the pond ecosystem, but they also give back to the energy grid through the house's geothermal and solar power systems and by not wasting any energy. Cutler's team dug 14 geothermal wells throughout the property. The design and engineering team are so confident in the integrity of the system that the wells have been buried and capped with four feet of soil.

In this geothermal system, a coil connected to a heat exchanger coils down hundreds of feet to the groundwater, which, in this part of Connecticut, is 12 degrees Celsius (54 degrees Fahrenheit). The heat exchanger uses the few degree temperature difference between the air and the groundwater to generate energy. In the winter, the clean energy warms the house and can heat its water supply up to 49 degrees Celsius (120 degrees Fahrenheit), Cutler explains. In the summer, the coil, which has been cooled by the groundwater, simply chills water blown against a fan, creating air conditioning.

In the summer, some 25,000 square feet (2,320 square meters) of PV panels, placed mostly on the garage, power the house and geothermal system and send surplus energy back to the grid. In the winter, the homeowners, instead, receive energy from the power company. Net-zero energy use is calculated over the course of a year, Cutler says. Batteries that store energy from the panels can also power the house for up to 20 days, as needed.

Cutler notes that there are trade-offs with geothermal systems. "There are higher up-front capital costs, but geothermal pays for itself through energy savings in eight to twelve years. The capital costs are about 50 percent more than a conventional HVAC system."

The residence was also designed for energy efficiency. Throughout the house, Cutler highly insulated the Douglas fir–clad rooms and hallways. While there is lots of glass, Cutler used one-inch-thick, triple-glazed insulated glass to cut back on heat loss and gain.

OPPOSITE **The bedrooms offer immersion in nature. Ceiling fans and operable windows allow the homeowners to reduce energy use.**

BELOW **Air conditioning and heating provided by the geothermal system come out of a subtle vent near the ceiling (upper left side of this image). In other parts of the house, vents are hidden inside the ceiling. All the Douglas fir floors have radiant heat, which the "dogs love," Cutler says.**

# Accord Passive House
Accord, New York, United States

**Peter Reynolds designed the Accord** Passive House, and he also lives in it. The 2,755-square-foot (256-square-meter) four-bedroom house was designed to be a demonstration project, to show the public and building-industry professionals that passive houses can be affordable, elegant, and low maintenance.

Reynolds is senior designer at North River Architecture and Planning, which has designed and built a series of passive house projects called FLEXHOUSE. According to Reynolds, his own certified Accord Passive House was constructed for under $300 per square foot. Given their simple shapes and details, the FLEXHOUSE can be built "competitively with conventional custom-home costs in the Hudson Valley," Reynolds explained in an interview.

He wanted to show that a "highly engineered certified passive house can feel artisanally designed and emotion-ally alive." The Accord Passive House achieves this by creating a sense of continuity with the local design language. The house's form refers to old Dutch barns, with their beautiful use of plain materials, that define the Hudson Valley. The frame is clad in simple, durable steel siding and reused oak and cork in the inside.

Incorporating passive house technologies also enabled Reynolds to break down the barrier between inside and outside, resulting in an "exuberant exposure to nature" within the house. In a conventional residence, a 20-by-20-foot (6-by-6-meter) glass wall would make a space feel very chilly in the winter. In this barn-style home, Reynolds was able to create a dramatic wall of triple-glazed glass where the barn door would be.

The magic of the home, says Reynolds, is that "I can be in my pj's on a winter day and sit right next to the window and feel perfectly comfortable." Due to the triple-glazed glass, super airtight building envelope, and heat-recovery ventilator—which filters, warms or cools, and then circulates fresh air every 20 minutes—the home seamlessly manages comfort levels year-round. "I never touch the thermo-stat; I never need to."

Because the house is about 80 percent more energy efficient than a conventional house, it can achieve net-zero energy use over the course of a year through rooftop PV panels with a 9-kilowatt capacity. The panels also ensure that the house is fully electric: the heating, cooling, electricity, and even transportation needs are powered by the panels, which create electricity during the day and exchange with the grid at night. Reynolds is able to plug his hybrid EV into the house's outdoor charger.

The Accord Passive House was designed for maximum flexibility. Reynolds lives only on the ground floor, which has retractable walls that open or close off areas to provide additional flexibility; the upper levels make up an unfinished attic space, which can be completed at a later stage.

Reynolds was also able to keep the costs down by building the Accord Passive House on the site of an abandoned shale pit. He mentioned that he purposefully seeks sites that require repair and restoration. The location seems like the perfect place for a regenerative home designed to achieve balance with the Hudson Valley's ecology and culture.

OPPOSITE **The 2,755-square-foot (256-square-meter) Accord Passive House achieves net-zero energy use by being 80 percent more energy efficient than a conventional house and incorporating rooftop PV panels with a 9-kilowatt capacity. The house is built on an abandoned shale bank.**

ABOVE  **In this Dutch barn-style home, a 20-by-20-foot (6-by-6-meter) glass wall takes the place of a barn door. The triple-glazed glass, very tight building envelope, and heat-recovery ventilator ensure a comfortable environment even on the coldest winter's day.**

OPPOSITE  **Light pours into the living room, creating the feeling that "you are camping indoors," says Reynolds. The fabric wall art above the sofa was created by DESIGNWORK, which makes zero-waste textiles from recycled Eileen Fisher clothes.**

LEFT  **Reynolds reused white-oak ceiling slats as door and window frames. Sliding pocket doors, seen here in red, enable maximum flexibility in opening and closing off spaces, creating privacy, as needed.**

OPPOSITE  **A guest room off of the kitchen shows how with passive houses there is no real trade-off between comfort and "an exuberant exposure" to nature.**

# Ex of In House
Rhinebeck, New York, United States

**Instead of letting 28 acres (11 hectares)** of forested rock outcroppings in Rhinebeck, New York, be broken up and turned into a five-house subdivision, architect Steven Holl decided to purchase the land and expand his experimental art and design community. The 28 acres have become the 'T' Space Nature Preserve, a complement to the original 'T' Space art gallery down the road. Within the site, the forest ecosystem of the Hudson Valley is largely conserved, with the exception of a few compact structures, such as a new library and archive, summer residents cabin, art installations, and a net-zero energy guesthouse called Ex of In.

In 2014, Steven Holl Architects began a research and development project focused on the "explorations of 'in'"—"in" relating to both interiors and the inversion of space. Holl states that in contrast to the typical spread-out house found in suburban sprawl, Ex of In House is about "compression and inner voids." In just 918 square feet (85 square meters), Holl plays with our sense of space, creating a generous volume by carving expansive orb forms inside the "tesseract trapezoidal" structure of the house and using unconventional window forms to bring the forest and sky inside.

But Ex of In isn't just an experiment in new building-landscape relationships, it's also a demonstration of innovative ways to use passive approaches and renewable energy systems to heat and cool a home and of an application of cutting-edge sustainable materials. Working with engineers at Transsolar, Holl and his team built one geothermal well that heats the two-story space with a concrete slab during cold seasons and ventilates and dehumidifies in the warmer seasons. The unconventional windows are designed to maximize solar heat gain in the winter but allow cross ventilation when opened during the summer. A wood-burning stove provides another heat source that spreads through the house.

The exterior is made of Poraver, a lightweight aggregate made of post-consumer recycled glass. The interior walls are made with a "super-insulated birch-plywood diaphragm construction." These forms are enriched by handcrafted mahogany window and doorframes and stairs.

One plane of the roof hosts thin-film SoloPower PV cells, which are connected to an energy-storage battery. At night, the battery powers the light fixtures, which are 3D printed in polylactic acid cornstarch-based bioplastics.

When an architecture fellow isn't in residence, Ex of In can be rented via Airbnb, with the proceeds going to the foundation. The listing notes that the woodstove is "highly efficient" in keeping the place warm in the winter. But the organic Japanese futons are on the firm side.

**The Ex of In House returns energy to the grid, relying on one geothermal well for heating and cooling and rooftop thin-film PV cells for energy.**

LEFT **One sleeping area showing the warm texture of the super insulated birch-plywood diaphragm construction. Holl states there are no distinct bedrooms, yet the house can sleep five. At left, a lamp made of PLA corn starch–based bioplastics is powered by the PV cells.**

OPPOSITE **In the winter, south-facing windows in the living room let the sun warm the space; in the warm months, screens can be pulled down.**

# Belfield Townhomes

Philadelphia, Pennsylvania, United States

In the Logan neighborhood of North Philadelphia, Onion Flats designed and built three affordable, four-bedroom townhouses as certified passive houses for $249,000 each. Green wall planters offer privacy on the front deck between the units.

**The US Department of Housing and** Urban Development (HUD) states that any family paying more than 30 percent of their income for housing is "cost burdened" and may not be able to afford basic necessities, such as food, clothing, transportation, and medical care. They estimate some 12 million American renters and homeowners now contribute more than 50 percent of their annual incomes toward housing.

The high cost of housing is in large part due to the lack of affordable, subsidized, or public housing in increasingly expensive urban areas, where nearly 80 percent of the US population lives. The National Low Income Housing Coalition stated that in 2018 approximately 7.2 million new affordable rental homes would be needed for people at or below the poverty level. According to the US Census Bureau, as of 2017, some 12.3 percent of the population, or nearly 40 million Americans, were at that level.

In the Logan neighborhood of North Philadelphia, which is a low-income and predominantly African American and Puerto Rican community, the developer Onion Flats helped expand the number of affordable-housing units by designing and building three 1,920-square-foot (178-square-meter) townhouses, each with four bedrooms.

When the houses opened in 2012, they were the first new affordable residences North Philadelphia had seen in five decades. They were also the first certified passive houses built in Philadelphia and Pennsylvania. Onion Flats codeveloped the townhouses with Raise of Hope (ROH), a local community-development corporation, for large, previously homeless families. What is also impressive is that Onion Flats built the three townhouses as passive houses in just three months at a cost of $249,000 each.

In 2010, the Philadelphia Office of Housing and Community Development approached Onion Flats to try to salvage a new affordable-housing development that had run into design and budgetary issues. The funding, earmarked through the Philadelphia Redevelopment Authority (PRA) and HUD, was, as noted by Onion Flats, "imminently at risk of being returned to HUD due to inaction." If they accepted the challenge of taking on the project with ROH, they had to agree to build the project just three months after the design and permitting process was complete.

HUD and PRA didn't require any sustainability measures, only that the townhouses had to be built for less than $129 per square foot. Onion Flats saw an opportunity to design a more energy-efficient and cost-effective building system, "one that was both radically unique and capable of meeting the Passive House building standard"

and also "based on everyday framing techniques [that are] easily transferrable to our trades." To reduce cost and speed up construction time, the firm partnered with a local modular factory that constructed the houses in prefabricated pieces that were then assembled on-site.

The need to keep costs low did not result in sacrificing sustainability performance or design quality. The passive townhouses include superinsulated walls, triple-pane windows, and a heat-recovery pump that draws in fresh air, filters it, and then efficiently heats or cools the air. Each house has rooftop PV panels with a 5-kilowatt capacity. If the tenants stay within their energy budgets, then the townhouses can produce as much energy as needed, making them net-zero in terms of energy use.

Onion Flats designed medium-density-fiberboard screens along the stairwell to add a playful element. Carbonized bamboo floors add some warmth. Tenants use energy-efficient induction cooktops and Bosch appliances.

According to the firm, the project became "the catalyst that inspired the Philadelphia Housing Finance Agency to begin to promote Passive House and net-zero energy building policies in their low-income-housing tax-credit program."

OPPOSITE  The townhouses were the first new affordable housing units in North Philadelphia in five decades. The roof of each energy-efficient townhouse is covered in PV panels with a capacity of 5 kilowatts.

RIGHT  The windows are protected from strong sun and glare by deep overhangs. Simple but elegant materials and finishes helped keep construction costs low. Carbonized bamboo floors create a sense of warmth.

BELOW  Belfield Townhomes are made of prefabricated modular components constructed in a nearby factory. Prefabrication reduces cost, improves efficiency, and means far less construction noise and disturbances to neighbors. A crane assembles the components on-site in a matter of days.

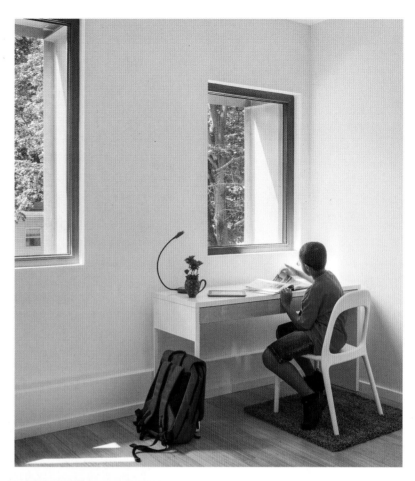

Onion Flats designed
medium-density-fiberboard
screens along the stairwell
to add a playful element
for kids.

# Paisano Green Community Senior Housing

El Paso, Texas, United States

The net-zero energy Paisano Green Community Senior Housing organizes 73 accessible units for low-income seniors around a central "tapestry garden" designed to bring the diverse community together.

**In 2010, the Housing Authority of** the City of El Paso (HACEP) in western Texas began deconstruction of an abandoned housing complex, recycling more than 90 percent of its materials for reuse in other projects. In its place, two years later, rose the first net-zero energy public-housing and senior-housing complex in the country.

On a 4.2-acre (1.6-hectare) site in the arid high-desert plateau, less than half a mile from one of the busiest border crossings between Mexico and the US, the Paisano Green Community Senior Housing project demonstrates that low-income seniors can have access to a sustainable, healthy home, in an affordable way. Only seniors and people with disabilities earning 30 percent or less of the annual median income qualify to lease one of the 73 accessible units.

WORKSHOP8, a Boulder, Colorado–based architecture firm, won the international design competition to design the super-energy-efficient LEED Platinum–certified complex, which they organized into five buildings that form a protective perimeter around a central "tapestry garden," a lush desert oasis designed by Desert Element Landscape Design and Indigo Landscape Design.

At the north end is a community center with a rooftop terrace, meeting rooms, a computer lab, and a communal kitchen; on the east edge of the site is a linear two-story building with nine single-room occupancies and nine one-bedroom units. In the western section, four three-story buildings contain 55 townhouses, consisting of one- and two-bedroom apartments.

The far-western edge of the three-story buildings is protected by a canopy wall clad in perforated metal panels that help insulate the complex from El Paso's powerful afternoon sun and cold winter winds.

Some 640 solar panels on the canopy wall and residential buildings take advantage of the three hundred days of sun El Paso receives a year, to produce 170 kilowatts of electricity. Two 60-foot-tall (18 meter) Xzeres 442SR wind turbines generate an additional 10 kilowatts. Together, these systems ensure the complex produces all the energy the community consumes in a calendar year.

Through a net-metering agreement with the Public Utility Commission of Texas, Paisano sells energy to the energy grid during the day at the same rate it purchases energy in the evenings, when the solar panels aren't generating electricity, thus using the grid as a battery. Some residents pay as little as $8 per month for energy.

But net-zero at Paisano wasn't achieved through the solar panels and wind turbines alone. WORKSHOP8 carefully oriented the buildings to optimize solar heat gain in the winter and minimize it in the summer.

Living units were designed to be insulated from the harsher effects of the surrounding environment. All residential buildings' roofs are coated in a high-albedo coating to reflect warming rays. The units themselves have "very tight envelopes" created with four different types of insulation. Their windows face north or south and are protected by sunshades, with windows facing south receiving extra protection from deep overhangs.

The units use both age-old techniques and inventive mechanical systems to take advantage of the sun and heat for heating and cooling. In the summer, the upper reaches of the units' 9- and 11-foot (2.7- and 3.3-meter) ceilings capture the warmer air and then ceiling fans help move that air out through upper-level windows. Mini-split-air-source heat pumps and energy-recovery ventilators circulate fresh air into the units and then capture energy from the expelled warm air. The air-source heat pumps also heat water in the units at a rate three times more energy efficient than conventional water heaters. The result: Paisano's homes are 85 percent more energy efficient than El Paso's current building-codes mandate. HACEP also holds monthly education seminars with residents, teaching them how to use the inventive mechanical systems in their homes and adapt their own behavior to reduce energy use.

The $14.8 million complex was financed with $8.25 million in grant funds from the federal American Recovery and Reinvestment Act of 2009, US Department of Housing and Urban Development Capital Fund Program grants, HACEP loans, and El Paso local government reserves.

HACEP estimates that Paisano Green Community Senior Housing cost approximately doubles the conventional public-housing project in El Paso, but will have a 20 percent lower cost to maintain over its 50-year lifespan. Furthermore, HACEP pays nothing for energy.

OPPOSITE **Two wind turbines and 640 PV panels on the rooftops of the residential buildings generate enough power for the entire complex. Energy efficiency guided the design of the units: windows face mostly south or north and have protective sunshades, with south-facing windows receiving extra protection from the sun through deep overhangs.**

RIGHT **Two 60-foot-tall wind turbines generate 10 kilowatts of power and make a powerful statement that Paisano Green Community Senior Housing is guided by an ethos of sustainability. The perforated metal-clad wall on the west edge of the complex protects against the strong setting sun and cold winds.**

# Grow Community
## Bainbridge Island, Washington, United States

LEFT  The solar-powered homes at the Village, which are seen in the foreground, are detached to provide light and air on all sides but are also close enough to each other to create a walkable community. Houses are rotated at an angle to ensure maximum privacy for homeowners.

OPPOSITE  The exteriors are clad in low-maintenance and durable prefabricated fiber-cement panels, sustainable locally harvested woods, and steel siding. Larger windows were placed on the south side of each house to maximize solar gain, while smaller windows on the north protect homeowners' privacy.

**"People want to live in a way that** reduces their carbon footprint. People are also tired of living in anonymous places; they want a sense of community. Net-zero energy communities provide both," explained Jonathan Davis, the architect who designed the first phase of Grow Community on Bainbridge Island, a ferry ride across Puget Sound from Seattle. According to Davis, models for walkable, socially enriching net-zero energy communities already exist; it's simply a matter of meeting demand and finding the right developers to build more of them.

The original phase of Grow Community, which is called the Village, was built in 2013 just as the building industry was coming out of the recession. While perhaps risky at the time, the development—which includes 22 closely packed, detached single-family houses, clustered into "microhoods" of six to eight houses, along with 20 apartments organized in two multifamily buildings—sold out in a year. The Village is about a 10-minute walk to downtown Winslow and the commuter ferry to Seattle.

Airtight building envelopes and thick layers of insulation help reduce energy use, which is offset by arrays of rooftop PV panels on the homes. "Residents who are conscious of their energy use can easily live within their energy budgets," says Davis.

Residents who purchased the 22 detached houses took out mortgages that not only covered the cost of the buildings, which ranged from $299,000 for a two bedroom to around $575,000 for a three bedroom, but also the cost of the rooftop solar arrays, which averaged $32,000 per home.

Davis, who owns a house in the Village himself, said a federal tax credit covered 30 percent of the cost of his solar panels, reducing the initial cost by more than $9,000. Washington State also offered an incentive of 54 cents for each watt of solar energy he produced. Given Davis generates up to 8 megawatts annually, he received a check for about $3,500 to $4,000 from the state each year. "After seven years, the solar panels paid for themselves, and I don't pay any energy bills." The entire development produces approximately 176 megawatts annually, meaning significant savings for all the homeowners.

Grow Community is one of the few in the US planned and designed with One Planet Living's 10 principles. Pooran Desai, a cofounder of Bioregional, a London-based development firm, started One Planet Living because he believed sustainability and well-being are inextricably linked. His approach has created communities that achieve not only net-zero energy use, but also zero waste, sustainable water use greater social interaction, food production, and lower greenhouse gas emissions from transportation.

Davis purposefully curved the paths, named Seed, Root, and Sprout, through the nearly 3-acre (1.2-hectare) site to encourage neighbors to interact. For the same reason, there are no parking spaces in front of homes. A common parking area next to the Village instead requires residents to walk through the community to their homes. "When I'm late for dinner, my wife knows that I bumped into a neighbor and got into a conversation," Davis said.

But perhaps the primary way the Village encourages a greater sense of community is the shared love for growing food. There are raised beds for vegetables and common gardens, which include blueberry bushes, strawberries, herbs, and apple trees. The 20 or so raised beds, located throughout the community, are used by almost all residents to grow vegetables, such as kale, cucumbers, carrots, and lettuces. The community, which includes retirees and empty nesters, singles and families with kids, organizes community dinners once or twice a year: "We harvest in the morning and eat together what we cooked that evening."

The second phase of Grow Community, designed by Bainbridge-based architect James Cutler, added another 5 acres (2 hectares), offering 50 townhouses and condominiums in multifamily buildings organized around central green spaces. Grow Community is now the largest planned net-zero community in Washington State.

For Davis, the lesson learned from the project is that "these communities aren't a big deal. Net-zero doesn't cost that much more. You just need to do some planning in advance."

The airtight building envelope, blow-in fiberglass insulation in the walls and attic, and double-glazed windows and sliding glass doors help significantly reduce energy use. These measures allow the home to be heated with just one mini-split ductless heat pump. A whole-house heat-recovery ventilator refreshes and distributes the air. Materials were selected for their low impact on the environment and human health. Interior floors are made of sustainable, renewable cork, and a recycled rubber and cork composite.

Almost all homeowners and renters in the Village community grow vegetables in the raised beds spread throughout the homes. While Davis doesn't call Grow Community an "agri-hood," as only a small portion of the total landscape is dedicated to food production, he argues that growing food together has not only helped build intergenerational community connections but also cut down on the greenhouse gas emissions associated with the transportation of food.

The Village's setup encourages low-carbon and social forms of transportation, like walking and bicycling, over getting in a car. The three main paths through the Village—Seed, Root, and Sprout—purposefully curve to encourage neighbors to bump into each other and start conversations. The parking lot is alongside the edge of the development.

# SolarCity Linz-Pichling
Linz-Pichling, Austria

**Linz is the third largest city in** Austria, with a population of approximately 200,000, and is the capital of the state of Upper Austria. In the 1980s, Linz mayor Franz Dobusch found that there was a sizeable gap between the number of jobs in the city and the city's population. This was leading to increasingly unaffordable housing costs within the city and the expansion of suburban sprawl, which causes long commutes and heavy traffic.

City leaders and planners developed a solution in the nearby Linz-Pichling district, which at the time was made up of lakes and riparian forests, degraded agricultural land, and a few single-family houses. In 1992, the State of Upper Austria and the City of Linz commissioned Austrian city planner Roland Rainer to create a low-energy and ecological city concept for four thousand mid- and low-income residents.

In 1994, the City of Linz convinced four leading nonprofit housing developers to finance the development of a city powered by solar energy, which would use both passive and active approaches to significantly reduce energy use. Leveraging €600,000 (US$675,000) in funds from the EU Directorate for Research and Development, they brought in architects Norman Foster, Richard Rogers, and Thomas Herzog, along with energy technology planner Norbert Kaiser, who together formed Renewable Energies in Architecture and Design (READ). This group was tasked with designing a community with 630 apartments and creating new breakthroughs in low-energy architecture design and construction. Two years later, an additional eight developers came on board, making it possible to create nearly 1,300 apartments on 79 acres (32 hectares). Viennese architect Martin Treberspurg won that commission.

During the same period, the city focused on how to eliminate any negative development impacts on the land—a strip of riparian forest surrounded by the Traun and Danube Rivers and adjacent to the Natura 2000 Traun-Donen-Auen nature preserve. Landscape architecture firm Latz + Partner created an initial plan that called for an additional 49 acres (20 hectares) of protected parkland. The plan formed the basis of a new competition that landscape architecture and urban design firm Atelier Dreiseitl won.

The €190 million (US$213 million) project was built over multiple phases starting in 2001. Approximately €125 million (US$140 million) was spent on the residential buildings and €65 million (US$73 million) for infrastructure and landscape. The first residents moved in 2003, and the new city was completed in 2005.

The developers and design team identified their approach to reducing energy use as *solar architecture*, which incorporates both passive and active strategies. On the passive side, each multistory apartment building is oriented south, and the distance between buildings is maximized for daylight. These approaches ensure that sunlight enters each living room, even during winter months.

According to the City of Linz, "the spectrum ranges from east-west-oriented deep structures with large-format windows to south-facing houses with six-meter-high winter gardens as a solar facade to passive houses in different designs." Windows also include an inventive "solarwave" honeycomb layer that is designed to absorb heat from solar rays in the winter and deflect solar rays in the summer; no external shades are needed.

On the active side, about 37,000 square feet (3,430 square meters) of rooftops were covered in PV panels. The panels meet approximately 50 percent of the electricity needed

OPPOSITE **SolarCity Linz-Pichling is one of the largest planned sustainable and ecological communities in the world. The apartment complexes radiate outward from a central commercial district and transportation hub that provides access to a tramline. Apartment complexes for four thousand residents are oriented south and separated far enough apart to enable all living rooms to receive sunlight, even during the winter months.**

for heating water. As for heating apartments in the winter, SolarCity relies on a highly energy-efficient district-heating system that is in part fueled by a biomass plant that generates both heat and electricity.

The community also reduces energy use from transportation. The compact neighborhoods were organized so residents can walk or bike to shops, the school, the kindergarten, and sports fields. The city extended a tramline into SolarCity, further reducing the need to use a car; every home is within 984 feet (300 meters) of a tram stop. Bus and rail connections are also nearby.

The entire development is rooted in an ecological approach. Atelier Dreiseitl came up with inventive ways to use green infrastructure to protect the watershed that supports the sensitive riparian forests; to expand the Kleiner Weikerslee lake by 70 percent, creating a natural swimming lake; to add a water playground and sports fields; and to bring the Aumühl, a 2.6-mile-long (4.2 kilometer) dry stream, back to life.

Artful and ecological ways to manage stormwater define the ambitious new city. Furthermore, the city uses an inventive wastewater-treatment system that captures and reuses urine as fertilizer and channels cleansed greywater back into the green spaces and the lake. Ultimately, as SolarCity expands, some 25,000 people are expected to call the community home.

LEFT **Nature is woven into daily life for the residents of SolarCity's highly energy-efficient apartments. Open channels and vegetated swales ensure all stormwater is captured where it falls, thereby protecting the water table and water quality in the floodplain and increasing local aquifer recharge, all of which supports the health of the surrounding riparian forest ecosystem.**

OPPOSITE TOP **Atelier Dreiseitl built small hills throughout the SolarCity landscape that create habitat for wildlife and also act as wind blocks that help reduce energy use. Some 1,500 trees were also planted to support those goals. In the background, PV panels cover an apartment building.**

RIGHT **Downtown SolarCity Linz-Pichling is filled with shops and restaurants. The rainbow-colored awnings represent the colors of the light spectrum, sending a clear public signal that the community is intimately connected with the movement of the sun and its energy-giving rays.**

FAR RIGHT **Life is fun in SolarCity Linz-Pichling! A bridge was designed just for the purpose of letting residents dive into the Klein Weikerlsee lake that was expanded 70 percent from the original lake to become a natural swimming lake. The landscape acts as a giant filter protecting the nearby Traun and Danube Rivers and the Natura 2000 Traun-Donen-Auen nature preserve from development impact.**

# Power of 10
## Örebro, Sweden

Power of 10 is organized into four row houses on an east–west orientation and six row houses on a north–south orientation. The roofs of the four houses on the east–west orientation are angled 45 degrees to the south to maximize the ability of the rooftop PV panels to generate electricity. These houses are coated in stucco, and the roofs are made of recycled steel.

**Örebro is 124 miles (200 kilometers)** west of Stockholm and is Sweden's sixth largest city, with a population of 125,000. This midsized European city is home to the appealing Power of 10, a series of 10 net-zero energy passive houses designed by Stockholm-based Street Monkey Architects. The Power of 10 demonstrates that highly energy-efficient dwellings are spreading far beyond capitals and major cities.

According to the International Passive House Association, there are now an estimated 30,000 passive houses across Europe. That number is expected to grow given the European Commission (EC)'s Energy Performance of Buildings Directive, which requires member states to create national regulations that ensure that all new buildings initiated after 2020 are nearly net-zero energy. Related EC directives call for decarbonizing all existing building stock through energy-efficiency improvements and the electrification of energy, heating, and cooling systems by 2050.

According to Cage Copher, a principal architect at Street Monkey, the set of generously sized 1,600-square-foot (148-square-meter) four-bedroom row houses are designed to accommodate "growing families." They are organized in an L-shape along two sides of a city block corner.

The architects wanted the roofs of all 10 row houses to face south so they could install rooftop PV panels that maximize energy generation. This was a challenge given that four houses are oriented east–west on one side of the corner, and six houses are oriented north–south on the other side. The solution was to angle the roofs south by 45 degrees on the four row houses with an east–west orientation and by 25 to 45 degrees on the six houses with a north–south orientation.

The result is the set of row houses generate 4 megawatt hours of electricity annually. Energy generated by the rooftop PV also powers EV chargers in the units' parking areas. Any excess energy is collected by each row house's 40-kilowatt battery cells. When the batteries are full, energy is sold to Örebro's grid.

According to the developer, Friendly Building, the PV panels were included in the overall price of the row houses. For all 10 row houses, "both energy production and consumption are measured. Energy use is paid by each house based on their consumption. Revenue from selling energy to the grid is divided equally. We would have made a bigger profit not installing solar cells and batteries, but we want to change the world, so it is worth less profit when you can do good."

Street Monkey Architects built the row houses out of prefabricated units made of recycled steel and also incorporated the material into the facades. Additionally, they simplified the design of the roofs to make the buildings more resilient to rain and snow. Copher says, "On the steel-covered gables of the group of four row houses, we do not use eaves, gutters, or downspouts. This way water can run down the side of the house without causing damage. On the group of six row houses, using steel allows us to integrate the gutters into the roof without an eave and recess the downspouts into the facade. Other materials would have been more vulnerable to water."

The houses were built to German passive house standards, so "they are airtight, well-insulated, and use a heat exchanger in order to reduce energy use for heating as much as possible. The houses require very little heat in the winter because of the construction."

Copher also argues there are clear benefits to designing and building net-zero energy passive homes through prefabrication: "There is a more efficient work flow with both labor and materials. We can ensure safer working conditions, which makes prefabrication faster and cheaper than on-site construction. Conflicts are typically found early in the building process and can be solved in a warm, safe environment. The process makes it easier to control quality and keep employees happy."

For the neighbors, the process is also a win. "With prefabrication, there is very little on-site disruption compared to on-site building. We had a crane there for a few days; then it is just finishing the work, which is neither messy nor noisy."

TOP **The rooftop PV panels generate 4 megawatt hours of electricity annually. The panels provide electricity to all of the houses in the Power of 10 development. Homeowners benefit from the sale of any excess energy back to Örebro's grid. Any energy-use costs are divided by homeowner based on consumption.**

BOTTOM LEFT **The design and construction team used a crane to assemble the core components of the prefabricated row houses in a matter of days, with little disruption to the neighbors. Finishing work is then completed on-site. Cage Copher, of Street Monkey Architects, argues that the process is more efficient, safer, and results in happier construction workers.**

BOTTOM RIGHT **EV chargers behind the row houses are covered in recycled Cor-Ten steel. The chargers are powered by Power of 10's rooftop PV panels or batteries.**

The interior of the prefabricated row house seems no different from one constructed on-site. The passive house design approach ensures a warm, cozy environment in the winter and ample light without solar heat gain in the summer.

The roofs of the six townhouses oriented north–south are angled 25 to 40 degrees to the south to optimize rooftop PV energy generation. These houses are clad in simple, durable materials, such as recycled steel. To add visual interest, alternating houses are covered in recycled Douglas fir-wood slats.

# Trent Basin
## Nottingham, United Kingdom

The sustainable residential community of Trent Basin will be built in five phases and will eventually result in 400 homes. Residents of townhouses and apartments in phase 2 of the development (seen here) enjoy views of the River Trent. A riverside promenade is lined with native plant meadows designed by Liz Lake Associates. The development is home to the shared garden (seen in the foreground) created collectively by the Trent Basin community and Blueprint to boost biodiversity and support social cohesion in this emerging neighborhood.

**In Nottingham, United Kingdom,** home of Robin Hood and Sherwood Forest, Trent Basin is a new community model that makes great strides toward achieving a future largely powered by renewable energy. With rooftop PV panels, a 2.1-megawatt-hour-capacity Tesla battery, and sophisticated energy-management software, the Trent Basin residential community has been able to generate and store its own energy, feeding directly into Great Britain's grid.

By connecting to the grid, the community energy system is able to trade energy generated on-site, selling stored energy to the grid when demand is high and storing excess power from the grid when public demand is low. This arbitrage provides an income to the Trent Basin Energy Services Company (ESCO), whose shareholders are made up of the University of Nottingham, the developer, and the residents of Trent Basin.

The community has become a virtual power plant—a decentralized energy source that supports grid resilience and stability, demonstrating that communities like Trent Basin can help solve the intermittency issues associated with greater reliance on wind energy, which is only generated when there is wind, and solar energy, which is only created when there is sunlight.

Just imagine hundreds of communities with their own energy-generation, storage, and management systems. With energy produced and stored close to where it is used and flowing in real time to meet demand and supply among a decentralized network, there would no longer be a need for centralized power plants transmitting power over long distances.

Some 128 miles (206 kilometers) north of London, Nottingham is the largest city in the East Midlands, with a population of 329,000. Since medieval times, the River Trent has been the lifeblood of the community. In the early 20th century, investments in improving navigability enabled barges to transport coal, petroleum, and building materials along the river. Nottingham became an inland port, and Trent Lane Depot a key interchange for goods coming into and heading out of the region.

But with the rise of rail and road networks in the 1960s and 1970s, river transportation fell out of favor, and the area became another underused industrial riverfront filled with toxic brownfields. Like so many cities, Nottingham has made the redevelopment of its riverfront central to its revitalization strategy.

Nottingham City Council established a 247-acre (100-hectare) waterside regeneration zone stretching along the north bank of the Trent, including the site of the former Trent Lane Depot, with the goal of better connecting inner-city neighborhoods along the river to the city center. Blueprint, a joint public-private partnership, has led the development of the Trent Basin community, which will provide four hundred new homes when complete. Trent Basin includes a mix of three-story townhouses, riverside houses, mews houses, and apartments at various prices designed for social diversity. The homes are set within a compact grid with small gardens.

A master plan for the £100 million (US$124 million) development created by urban planners at URBED, architects at Marsh:Grochowski, and landscape architects at Liz Lake Associates was approved in 2014. The plan envisions a walkable, sustainable residential community built in five phases over a decade. The first two phases have been completed, and the third phase, which was designed by Sarah Wigglesworth Architects, is now in development.

Phase 1, which opened in 2016 and quickly sold out, included 45 low-energy homes maximized for light and views, with double- or triple-glazed windows, high levels of insulation, and low-energy appliances. Phase 2 included 31 homes, a mix of two-to-four-bedroom homes ranging from £195,000

Phase 1 of the development, designed by Marsh:Growchoski, included 45 low-energy homes set within a compact district that privileges pedestrians and bicyclists. Streets widen at certain points to form civic spaces.

(US$242,000) to £450,000 (US-$560,000). Phase 3 includes an additional 33 homes along a new street connected to the basin front. The homes are designed to meet enhanced energy-performance standards, improving on the requirements stipulated by UK building regulations by roughly 20 to 30 percent.

Homeowners are connected to the conventional energy grid, and are all able to join Sustainable Community Energy Networks (SCENe), a pilot program financed by Innovate UK and made possible through a consortium of private, public, and academic partners, including the University of Nottingham, SmartKlub, Solar Ready, and Blueprint.

Those who sign on to SCENe receive a smart meter and access to energy-management apps that enable them to track energy use in their home and across the network and better manage their own energy demand. As Professor Mark Gillott, the academic head of SCENe at the University of Nottingham, told the *Engineer*: "The system had to be smart, easy, and hassle-free for consumers to use, so the benefits are clear to other developers and the system will get more traction."

PV panels, which serve the community energy battery, are located on viable homes and are subject to a "rent a roof" agreement with ESCO, which is, in turn, responsible for their maintenance and management. The PV panels are a community asset rather than the property of an individual household. A company called Limejump uses a trading platform to buy and sell Trent Basin's energy to the grid. The SCENe ESCO returns profits from energy sales to homeowners.

Gillott added that the system is designed to be fully responsive: "Could we get better value from trading with the grid at this time? Or could [the system] be best used for vehicle charging, heat generation, or local use? It's about optimizing the use of local energy assets while integrating with the national grid to get best value from them. In the future, we want to do some of this in-house, using machine learning and some of our own bespoke algorithms to allow us to trade energy locally."

The *Engineer* reports that since SCENe went online in 2018, the system has "saved 110 tons of carbon dioxide, generated over 310,000 kilowatt hours of renewable energy, offset energy costs for householders, and created a new company and business model that is attracting interest from more housing developers."

The development is also planned and designed to reduce energy use from transportation. Homeowners are allocated one parking space or shared street parking and benefit from discounted access to a car club. In 2018, the UK office of low-emission vehicles offered a 75 percent discount to homeowners at Trent Basin who install EV charging ports. The development is also near a new dedicated bike path and electric bus lane.

In 2018, Lord Henley, the Parliamentary Under Secretary of State at the Department for Business, Energy and Industrial Strategy, ceremonially switches on the 500-kilowatt Tesla lithium-ion community battery, which can store up to 2.1 megawatt hours of energy. At the time, the battery was the largest community storage system in Europe. The battery could power 660 homes simultaneously for one hour.

ABOVE **Phase 2 of the development, designed by Marsh:Growchoski and Sarah Wigglesworth Architects, features the simple forms of vernacular Nottingham architecture. According to Wigglesworth,** the repeated pitched roofs take "their form from red brick factory style buildings." Rear patios and backyards bring air and light to homeowners but also ensure the development remains compact and walkable.

OPPOSITE **Homes facing the street also have small patios lined with trees and shrubs. Windows are double or triple glazed and are designed to reduce thermal bridging, improving the energy efficiency of the homes by 20 to 30 percent over what is stipulated by UK building regulations.**

# Zero Carbon House
Birmingham, United Kingdom

**Zero Carbon House, the most sustainable house in the United Kingdom, features a contemporary addition, covered with PV panels and solar water heaters, grafted onto the side of a two-bedroom house from the 1840s.**

**Before leaving office in 2019, British** prime minister Theresa May put into law an ambitious target for the United Kingdom: carbon neutrality by 2050. This action made the UK the first major economy in the G7 to legislate net-zero greenhouse gas emissions. Given 40 percent of the UK's emissions are from its buildings, local governments have been ratcheting up performance goals for both new buildings and the retrofits of older buildings. West Midlands county, Birmingham—the second largest city in the UK with a population of 1.1 million—has set a goal of net-zero by 2030. There, architect John Christophers has shown the way forward with his own home, the Zero Carbon House.

Christophers built an extension to his circa-1840 two-bedroom terraced brick house. Where there was once a garage, Christophers built a two-story contemporary add-on with a kitchen, dining room, and high-ceilinged living room with a skylight. On the second floor, a new studio space called the long room is found under a sloping roof that holds PV panels and solar water heaters. According to Christophers: "The long room roof is at the right height, pitch, and orientation for the solar panels."

While that seems conventional enough, Christophers took the opportunity to rethink all the systems in the older building and achieve an expanded energy-positive house. The original

1840s house was estimated to release 46,200 pounds (21,000 kilograms) of carbon dioxide each year. The new Zero Carbon House is carbon positive, creating more energy than it uses for a net reduction of 1,300 pounds (660 kilograms) of carbon dioxide annually. The house was the first and only retrofit in the UK to reach Level 6 of the Code for Sustainable Homes, and Christophers won the prestigious RIBA Architecture Award in 2010 for his efforts.

Christophers incorporated a number of smart and artful energy-saving strategies: "The entire home is lined with a membrane like a giant balloon," which is designed to stop air and heat from escaping in the winter, thereby reducing the need for heating energy. The floors are made of rammed earth pulled from the foundation of the house mixed with red clay. "This material is so dense that it holds the heat of the house, keeping us warm in the winter and cool in the summer."

As for wall insulation, Christophers took a customized approach: "The old and new walls at the side and back of the house are insulated on the outside. The insulation is a material called Neopor, a bit like polystyrene but using graphite, which reflects radiant heat back into the house. The front of the old house has lovely historic brick-and-stone features, so we chose to insulate the walls internally with Warmcel 500, an insulation material made from

recycled cellulose fiber—old newspapers. It's 16 times better at keeping the heat in than before." Windows throughout were replaced with triple-glazed ones with double air seals around the edges. "They are 14 times better at insulating than the original single glazing."

On the roof, there are Consolar UK vacuum-tube solar panels that heat up water, which is stored in a hot-water cylinder five times the size of a conventional one. Additional PV panels generate 5 kilowatts of energy. Christophers uses a monitoring system that tells him how much hot water and electricity he has at any given point.

On the rare occasion when the solar panels are covered in snow in the winter, and therefore not generating energy for the hot-water cylinder, Christophers takes a few dead branches harvested off the ash tree in his garden and feeds them into a wood-burning stove. Heat from the stove warms the house and the hot-water storage system, so no heat energy is wasted. On the coldest days, "the wood-burning stove needs to be lit for a few hours only, every two-to-three days."

A few other noteworthy aspects: Rainwater collected from the roof reduces water use by 50 percent. There are 14 reclaimed materials throughout the house. And 99 percent of construction waste was recycled.

OPPOSITE  **A view into the rear of the house, which faces south and west, shows where the original house was fused to the new addition. Triple-glazed windows boost energy efficiency. At left in the interior, the brick walls of the older house add warmth to the dining room and living room. The superinsulated structure is clad in simple white with dashes of color.**

BELOW  **The charming dining room flows into the kitchen that features an induction cooktop stove. According to John Christophers, "We cook with the renewable electricity generated by our PV panels. Our induction cooktop works by inducing a magnetic field in the stainless steel–bottomed saucepans and is two to three times more efficient than most electric cooktops. It also has the advantage of being as responsive as gas and very safe because there's no flame or hot ring."**

RIGHT  **A peek inside a wall panel shows the heat exchanger: a mechanical ventilation heat recovery system (MVHR). Christophers explained: "Warm humid air is extracted from the bathrooms and kitchen and discharged outside—but the MVHR doesn't take the heat with it. Over 90 percent of the heat from the outgoing air is recovered and prewarms the air that is coming in, which is ducted to reach every room. It also filters atmospheric grime from the incoming air. Although the MVHR uses some electricity, it saves several times more energy than it uses."**

At left, the sloping ceiling of the long room work space has just the right height, pitch, and orientation for the PV panels and solar water heaters found on the roof above. Zero Carbon House relies on a series of charming windows of different sizes for natural ventilation during the spring, summer, and autumn. The earth in the rammed-earth floors was pulled from the foundation of the home and mixed with red clay and beeswax. The artwork is Space & Circumference by Jake Lever.

# M-KOPA Solar
## Nairobi, Kenya

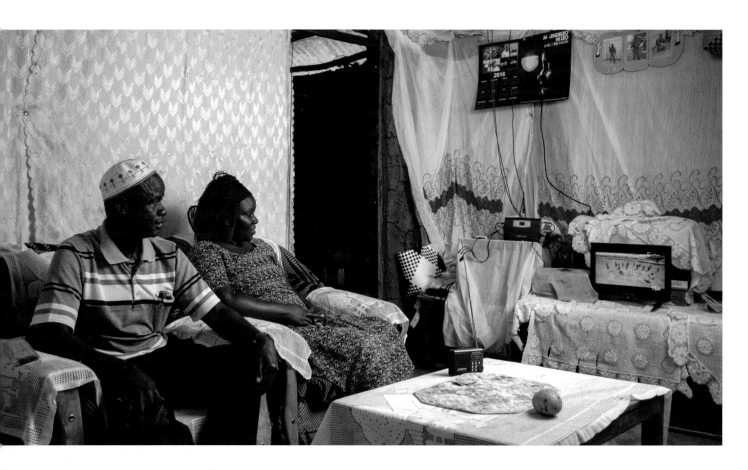

A couple in Western Kenya watch their TV, powered by rooftop PV panels. To date, **M-KOPA** has sold **100,000** solar TV systems, which means **500,000** more people have access to news and information.

**Of the 1.25 billion people who live in** Africa, approximately half live off the energy grid. And of the 1 billion people who live in sub-Saharan Africa, some 60 percent live in rural areas where access to the grid is either very expensive or nonexistent. For millions of households, one of the few options for lighting has been lamps fueled by paraffin or kerosene, which are relatively expensive, produce low quality light, and emit particulate matter and noxious chemicals linked with asthma and lung cancer.

One way to bring electricity and light to communities with no grid connection is through rooftop PV panels. Depending on how many watts of electricity they generate, PVs can power lights, cell phones, radios, TVs, and more.

To bring the opportunities that electricity provides to low-income households in cities and rural areas, Jesse Moore, Nick Hughes, and Chad Larson founded M-KOPA Solar in 2010 in Nairobi, Kenya. Ten years later, M-KOPA has provided affordable off-grid PV power solutions to 750,000 homes in Kenya, Uganda, Tanzania, and Nigeria—or an estimated 3.5 million people. *MIT Technology Review* called M-KOPA one of the 50 smartest companies in the world.

The collective power produced by these homes is an estimated 1.85 megawatts, which is equal to saving 150,000 tons of greenhouse gas emissions from entering the atmosphere each year. Power from these panels has meant 93.8 million hours of kerosene-free lighting each month. M-KOPA also states that their system costs less than kerosene.

M-KOPA offers a range of products and services. The simplest and lowest-cost home system includes one 8-watt solar panel, a solar rechargeable FM/USB radio, one lithium battery, four 1.2-watt LED bulbs, one five-in-one phone charger cable, a custom cable, and a solar rechargeable LED torch. The most comprehensive options also include features like a 60-watt PV panel, 32-inch flat-screen TV with remote control and antenna, a satellite dish, and a cooling fan.

Using Safaricom's M-Pesa, a mobile phone–based money transfer service that is available throughout East Africa, M-KOPA customers pay an initial deposit of approximately US$35 and then a daily installment of approximately US$0.50 to US$1 over two years. After that period, the customer owns the system.

Customers can pick up the system at one of 70 service centers operated by local technicians, including women and youth who are being trained for Africa's growing technology-based economy. The system comes with a control box, which has a SIM card that communicates with the customer's mobile-payment account. If customers fall behind on their daily payments, the control box pauses the system until they can catch up.

According to M-KOPA, no collateral is needed. Customers only need their national ID card and matching mobile money account. M-KOPA offers a three-year warranty on its control unit, bulbs, TV, and solar panels, and a two-year warranty on the chargers and cables. Upgrades and cash loans are available to customers with good repayment records. The company states that more than 90 percent of its customers have repaid.

In 2016, M-KOPA began sourcing 20-watt and 15-watt panels at the Solinc East Africa factory in Naivasha, Kenya, to reduce the cost of panels to customers. Two years later, the company had sold over 100,000 PV panels made locally, supporting the growing African renewable energy economy. The goal is to source 500,000 panels that can generate 6.6 megawatts of power locally over the next two years.

Dorothy Nabawesi, who bought the M-KOPA 400 system at the company's shop in Mukono, Uganda, told the company: "I don't have the money to access the grid. For so long, the good things have been passing me by, like watching national and international news on TV. My grandchildren used to go to a neighbor's house to get information about the world. Now with M-KOPA, I have better lighting for them to read, plus extra power to charge my phone, listen to radio, and watch TV." To date, M-KOPA has sold 100,000 solar TV systems, which means an estimated 500,000 more people have access to news and information.

ABOVE  **A family in Western Kenya enjoys dinner together under an LED light powered by an M-KOPA home system.**

LEFT  **Watching Nipashe Michezo, local sports news in Kenya.**

**An M-KOPA** sales field agent installs a satellite dish on the roof of a customer's house. **M-KOPA** hires employees from the communities in which they sell their products, training workers for sub-Saharan Africa's burgeoning green-tech economy.

**An M-KOPA** employee helps a customer sign a contract for **M-KOPA Solar** services. All customers need are their national identification cards and an **M-PESA**-registered line.

# SMA x ECO TOWN Harumidai
Sakai City, Japan

**Daiwa House Industry Company,** founded in 1955, is one of Japan's largest home builders. The company became famous in the late 1950s for designing one of the first compact prefabricated houses built in post–World War II Japan. Over the ensuing decades, Daiwa House expanded into hotels, resorts, single-family houses, and commercial properties in Japan, Southeast Asia, Oceania, and North America.

Daiwa House is now shifting its focus to prefabricated communities that produce more energy than they use—they are energy positive. In 2011, in Senboku New Town, Sakai City, Osaka prefecture, the company proposed building a model ecotown. Two years later, they created the SMA x ECO TOWN Harumidai, a 4-acre (1.6-hectare) development on the site of a former elementary school, which includes 65 energy positive single-family houses, each approximately 1,250 square feet (117 square meters), and a community center. By the end of 2017, SMA x ECO TOWN Harumidai produced 427 megawatt hours of clean energy, 15 percent more energy than it used, reducing its carbon emissions from electricity generation by an estimated 95 percent.

Wakihama Naoki, from the firm's Osaka urban-development office, told *Japan Journal* that Daiwa House founder Ishibashi Nobuo predicted the need for energy-positive homes in the mid-1990s, before the climate crisis was widely acknowledged: "He was the first man to point out that wind, the sun, and water would be the three essential factors for our company's business in the 21st century."

Given the ever-present fear of major earthquakes, like the Great East Japan Earthquake that hit Japan in 2011, Daiwa House built each house so it was not only energy-positive but also resilient. Each house is both a self-sustaining power plant and a storage facility: energy produced through a 5-kilowatt rooftop array of PV panels is stored in a 6.2-kilowatt lithium-ion battery, the product of ELIIY Power Company. An "Ene-Farm" fuel cell provides an additional energy source. Each home also has a cistern to collect and store rainwater.

The community center doubles as a disaster-preparedness and disaster-relief hub. Public spaces host arrays of PV panels that generate total of 19.6 kilowatts of power for shared infra-structure, like streetlights. A central 14.7-kilowatt lithium-ion battery stores energy that can be used in a time of crisis. Furthermore, an estimated 24 kilowatts of energy stored within the batteries of the community's shared EVs can be accessed through the community center's parking garage, providing another backup power source: "We are prepared for energy emergencies."

Achieving an energy-positive state took more than just PV panels and batteries. To reduce the need for air conditioning in the summer, Daiwa House ran simulations to determine how to best lay out the development in order to maximize the cooling benefits of the surrounding forest to the south and east and the winds that blow across a reservoir inside the town. Daiwa House planted street trees outside residences and along each road and covered all common buildings and retaining walls in greenery. According to the company, the presence of nearby nature also "enhances the residents' attachment to the town and enriches everyone's lives."

To reduce the need for air conditioning in the summer, the 65 energy-positive homes of SMA x ECO TOWN Harumidai were organized to maximize cooling breezes from the surrounding forest and a reservoir inside the town.

The houses themselves incorporate a range of passive-energy efficiency approaches—from tight building envelopes and thick insulation to LED lights, "wind catcher" windows that promote ventilation, and custom thermal insulation window screens that can block 70 percent of solar radiation.

Homeowners use the company's proprietary home-energy-management system, a data dashboard called D-HEMS, that automatically moves energy into storage for use at night and enables homeowners to track how much energy they are generating and using. The company states that "each family's share in the community's energy-conservation efforts is displayed in a ranking. Families with a high ranking are awarded points they can use for the electric-vehicle car-sharing service." Daiwa House estimates the shared EVs are used 250 times annually. As an added incentive to conserve energy, profits from excess energy sold by the community to the grid are returned to the homeowners' association.

The 65 homes within the development sold out in 2014, with each selling for approximately ¥47 million (US $435,000). Daiwa has since built six more ecotowns using the same model. Other Japanese conglomerates, including Panasonic, are creating similar communities across Japan and Southeast Asia.

**To optimize energy production, PV panels are primarily placed on the south side of the roofs.**

ABOVE **Daiwa House Industry Company buried all the electricity and utility lines and incorporated trees and plants to create a more natural, pleasing residential environment. One resident says, "I like the fact that there are no utility poles in the streets. The roads are wide, and there is a beautiful townscape. Children have started to want to play outside."**

LEFT **The community center charges EVs from a lithium-ion battery that receives electricity from rooftop PV panels.**

# The Sustainable City
Dubai, United Arab Emirates

In the aftermath of the 2008 financial crisis, Diamond Developers, based in the United Arab Emirates (UAE), did a complete about-face, transforming itself from a traditional developer into one aiming for sustainable-design excellence. Cofounders Faris Saeed, a trained civil engineer, and his architect partner Wassim Adlouni, spent four years traveling the world studying sustainable communities to find out what was working and what wasn't. Saeed commented, "Each community we visited focused on one thing—energy, waste, or farming. Most didn't innovate on the social part or study the commercial side enough. To make a project sustainable, you have to combine three elements—environment, society, and economics—together."

The result of their deep investigations is the nearly net-zero energy Sustainable City in Dubai, which opened in 2016 at a cost of AED 1.3 billion (US$354 million) and where three thousand people from 64 countries now live. The developers took a holistic approach to sustainability by designing a community that can produce its own food, creating access to nature and outdoor exercise opportunities, conserving and reusing water, reducing waste, and offsetting 87 percent of its energy use through rooftop PV panels that generate 7.47 gigawatt hours of energy annually.

They also organize 265 annual events, including yoga classes, fitness challenges, exhibitions, outdoor movie nights, and food-production workshops, to engender a sense of community among the diverse residents. According to Saeed, it has ranked as the "happiest community" in the UAE for the third year in a row.

The 114-acre (46-hectare) Sustainable City is organized into a grid enclosed by a buffer zone of 2,500 100-foot-tall (30 meter) trees interlocked in layers to block out air pollution. This buffer zone also doubles as an exercise space, with a 2.5-mile (4-kilometer) two-way cycling track and 1.8-mile (2.9-kilometer) walking path.

Within the grid, five hundred villas are organized into five residential clusters arrayed along a central green spine that includes constructed lakes and an urban farm with 11 temperature-controlled "biodome" greenhouses, which provide 32,000 square feet (3,000 square meters) of space for growing 36 types of organic vegetables and herbs. Shared food production is seen as central to forging bonds among the residents.

There are also 89 apartments in a central mixed-use district near the entrance of the city, which includes shops and restaurants. Other central nodes include the Fairgreen International School, Sanad Autism Village, the Innovation Centre, the Equestrian Club, and the Mosque.

Along with trees and the urban farms, Diamond Developers used a variety of strategies to help reduce the urban heat-island effect and, therefore, the residential energy use. The clusters are oriented to capture 85 percent of prevailing winds. The central urban plaza also includes strategically placed Barjeel wind towers that help cool the streets. Temperatures can be anywhere from 1 to 16.5 degrees Celsius (2 to 30 degrees Fahrenheit) lower than surrounding areas.

The three-bedroom L-shaped villas—which can either be purchased

The 114-acre Sustainable City in Dubai uses rooftop PV panels on both homes and common spaces to generate 1.7 gigawatt hours of renewable energy annually. Running roughly top to bottom in the center of this image are solar panel–covered car parks with EV charging stations. Running left to right is the central green spine with urban farms and 11 biodome greenhouses.

for around AED 3 million (US$817,000) or rented for AED 13,500 (US$3,800) a month—were designed to maximize daylight by orienting windows north while reducing solar heat gain. Each home, which includes a range of energy-efficient measures, including tight envelopes, insulation, LED lights, and low-energy appliances, are covered in rooftop PV panels that offset 50 percent of energy use.

Common areas are also put to work to generate power. Each cluster has a parking garage covered in PV panels with chargers for EVs. The developers ensured that no parking garage was farther than 280 feet (85 meters) from any home. For those without cars, the community provides access to free electric-powered buggies. Even the gym, which gets more than 13,000 visits a year, leverages customized stationary ellipticals, treadmills, and bikes to produce 152,000 kilowatt hours of human-generated energy a year.

Diamond Developers claim that between the energy-efficiency measures and the PVs, the average homeowner and renter saves anywhere from AED 7,454 (US$2,000) to AED 16,900 (US$4,600) in annual energy costs. The entire development offsets some 8,500 tons of carbon dioxide equivalent each year.

LEFT **Because cars are housed in central parking lots adjacent to the homes, the streets are safe for walking and bicycling. The entire development is oriented to capture 85 percent of prevailing winds, reducing the urban heat-island effect.**

OPPOSITE **Amid lush plants and trees that help to cool the air, the city's L-shaped three-bedroom energy-efficient villas offset 50 percent of their energy use through rooftop PV panels.**

# Chapter Two

# POWER COMMUNITY SPACES

## Power Community Spaces

—

## Parks, Transportation, and Sports Centers

Our communities are made up of shared spaces and infrastructure. We rely on transportation systems for our economic, cultural, and social life. We need local parks and green streets more than ever to get out of our homes, socialize, and experience the health benefits of nature. We have sports centers to exercise, build character, and strengthen community bonds.

Our community infrastructure shapes our identity and values, so it's important that these spaces signal that renewable energy is becoming an integral part of our community life. By generating renewable energy and reducing community energy use, these spaces can also make real—not just symbolic—contributions to our environment, health, and well-being. Power Community Spaces showcases sustainably powered community spaces around the world that demonstrate smart design of shared infrastructure moves renewable energy forward.

Power plants and buildings account for large shares of greenhouse gas emissions. But it may be surprising to learn that emissions from the transportation sector, which are produced by burning fossil fuels for cars, trucks, buses, ships, planes, and trains, account for 15 percent of emissions worldwide. In the developed world, the numbers are even higher. According to the Environmental Protection Agency, nearly 30 percent of all greenhouse gas emissions in the US is produced by the transportation sector. In Europe, the share is approximately the same.

We can address this challenge by making renewable energy the only source of our electricity and electrifying transportation systems. All electric cars, trucks, buses, and light-rail would improve energy efficiency and eliminate greenhouse gas emissions from the transportation sector. They would also make our air much cleaner, preventing hundreds of thousands of premature deaths from air pollution each year.

According to a 2019 article by Niklas Höhne and others in the scientific journal *Nature*, "21 countries, 5 regions, and more than 52 cities have committed to make all vehicles emission-free." Many more countries and cities need to jump on board.

More electric vehicles (EVs) on our roads means more EV chargers and investment in EV battery and charger technology. The time it takes to charge an EV has been rapidly decreasing—new superfast chargers are capable of fully powering up an EV in as little as eight minutes. Two EV charging stations—one in Hangzhou, China, and another in Fredericia, Denmark—have shown that station design is critical to expanding the use and social acceptance of EVs and public-charger infrastructure.

We can also strengthen a community's sense of pride and connection with renewable energy by designing it into central community hubs, namely parks and sports centers. Amager Bakke, familiarly known as CopenHill, in Copenhagen, Denmark, is a waste-to-energy power plant topped with a park and sports center, with nature areas, hiking trails, and a ski slope open year-round. The facility is multifunctional community infrastructure that both reflects and promotes the Danes' core environmental values.

In Washington, DC, Washington Canal Park shows the potential for parks to become central nodes in networks of EV chargers and to reduce energy use through geothermal sources. The National Stadium in Kaohsiung, Taiwan, a photovoltaic-covered sports center shaped like a coiled dragon, is set within a lush urban park. These designs all show how nature makes renewable energy even more appealing.

# Washington Canal Park
## Washington, DC, United States

LEFT  **Washington Canal Park in southwest Washington, DC, is one of the first parks to use a geothermal heating and cooling system to reduce energy use. The park's renewable energy system saves some $25,000 in utility costs annually.**

OPPOSITE  **Because of subpar soil quality, the design and construction team needed deep piles and subsurface construction to support the ice-skating rink and pavilion (at left), which houses a café and bathrooms. The team leveraged the network of piles to create 28 geothermal wells that provide heating and cooling for the pavilion.**

**Washington Canal Park in Washington**, DC, uses 28 geothermal wells to reduce the energy use of the park by 12 percent. While the park isn't net-zero in terms of its energy use, it demonstrates the great potential for public spaces to incorporate geothermal heating and cooling. Plus, four EV chargers on its perimeter show how public spaces can support sustainable transportation.

The 3-acre (1.2-hectare), three-block-long park, which opened in 2012, replaced a district school-bus parking lot. Before it was paved over in the early 1900s, the land was part of the Washington City Canal, which connected the Anacostia and Potomac Rivers. According to landscape architecture firm OLIN, the $27 million park is meant to evoke that historic waterway with a "linear rain garden reminiscent of the canal, and three pavilions, which recall

floating barges that were once common." Together with STUDIOS Architecture, OLIN designed the park to be an inclusive mecca for the Southeast DC community, which had long been underserved in terms of green space. The park is adjacent to a low-income public housing community, creating a significant new amenity for the residents.

Down the middle of the linear park are spaces to lounge on lawns, dotted with metal, kinetic sculptures by David Hess. There are curved benches set within wild native and adapted grasses. In the summer, play fountains draw kids to the park; while in the winter, families loop along the ice-skating rink. The rink area is flanked by a pavilion with a café covered by a publicly accessible green roof. The green roof features what must be a first: signs letting people know to curb their dogs around the sedum.

While the geothermal system is invisible to everyday visitors, Skip Graffam, a partner and director of research at OLIN, sees the value of the approach. Graffam argues that "all landscape architects should strive to reduce energy demand in their projects and look for creative opportunities to achieve on-site energy generation and/or storage." He believes the best way to prevent these features from being cut later during the commissioning process is by working across disciplines "to find the most cost-efficient solution that addresses multiple project requirements and providing clear and rigorous life-cycle performance and benefit analysis to the client."

In the case of Washington Canal Park, subpar soil conditions forced the design and construction team to incorporate piles and subsurface

LEFT  The park is a respite in DC's humid summers. Trees provide shade and cool the air, while native and adapted plants add a flash of color and support pollinators. The end result is an inviting place to sit.

BELOW  The shallow water channel running through the linear park evokes the site's past as part of the Washington City Canal, which once connected the Anacostia and Potomac Rivers. One pavilion is clad in sustainably harvested black locust wood, an American alternative to tropical hardwoods like ipe. Where the park meets the street, there is one of the EV chargers that can be accessed with a swipe of a credit card.

POWER COMMUNITY SPACES

construction in order to support the ice rink and pavilion. At the same time, the café and bathrooms in the pavilion needed a heating and cooling system. With these two requirements, it made financial sense to leverage the foundational columns, which had to be driven into the ground, for a geothermal ground-source heating and cooling system for the pavilion. This smart approach saves approximately $25,000 in utility costs each year. "This degree of cost savings can free up financial resources for the benefit of events and operations," says Graffam.

The park is the result of a public-private partnership between developer WC Smith, which created the nonprofit Canal Park Development Association (CPDA); the Anacostia Waterfront Corporation, a government-owned corporation; and the government of the District of Columbia. Everyone involved wanted to make the park a showcase of sustainable landscape design. Former CPDA executive director Chris VanArsdale said his group pushed hard for incorporating geothermal heating and cooling, the EV chargers, and a range of other sustainable features. For example, the pavilions, which were designed by STUDIOS Architecture, are clad in reclaimed and sustainably harvested wood from black locust trees, which is a great alternative to unsustainable rainforest hardwoods, like ipe and cumaru.

Washington Canal Park also incorporates a complex green infrastructure system comprising rain gardens, deep spaces around trees, and 80,000-gallon (302,000-liter) underground cisterns that collect, manage, and treat almost all stormwater landing on the park, as well as rooftop runoff channeled from surrounding residential and office buildings, about 1.5 million gallons (5.6 million liters) annually. Treated water is then reused to satisfy up to 95 percent of the park's needs for foundations, irrigation, toilets, and the ice-skating rink.

Because of all these inventive elements, Washington Canal Park was one of the first parks to be certified with three stars by the Sustainable SITES Initiative's pilot program. Today, the park is maintained by the Capitol Riverfront Business Improvement District on behalf of the nonprofit Canal Park and brings in musicians like funk star George Clinton for free summer concerts.

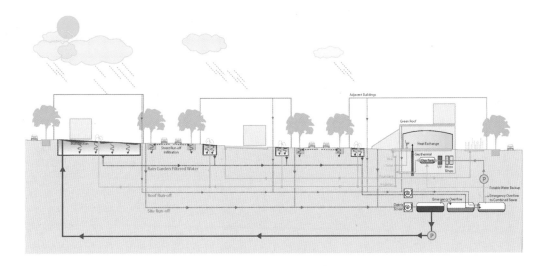

This diagram shows the incredible engineering below the surface. An elaborate system of rain gardens, deep tree pits, and 80,000-gallon (302,000-liter) underground cisterns help collect, manage, and treat some 1.5 million gallons (5.6 million liters) of stormwater from the park and nearby buildings. At right, the diagram depicts the geothermal system that leverages the deep piles beneath the pavilion.

# Amager Bakke (CopenHill)
Copenhagen, Denmark

Amager Bakke is a US$660 million waste-to-energy power plant topped in an astroturf-covered ski slope and hiking trails. Some 400,000 tons of garbage is incinerated by two furnaces at 1,000 degrees Celsius (1,830 Fahrenheit) to generate electricity and district heating.

**A decade ago, Danish architect** Bjarke Ingels came up with a fantastical idea: to build a ski slope on top of a power plant. Well, now, it has actually happened. The US$660 million Amager Bakke is now welcoming adventurous ski bunnies in Copenhagen, Denmark.

Known to locals as CopenHill, this cutting-edge, 441,000-square-foot (40,900-square-meter) facility converts waste into energy and heat while giving sports lovers access to a 1,480-foot-long (450 meter) ski slope, a 280-foot-high (85 meter) climbing wall, and 1,600-foot-long (490 meter) hiking and running trail designed with SLA, a landscape architecture firm. The project is the most visible demonstration yet of Copenhagen's ambition to become a carbon-neutral city by 2025.

According to Babcock & Wilcox Vølund, the engineers of the power plant, Amager Bakke will convert 400,000 tons of waste each year into heat for 160,000 households and electricity for another 62,500 while eliminating 99.95 percent of toxic sulfur dioxide and reducing nitrogen-oxide emissions by 90 percent. Depending on local heat and electricity demand and prices, Amager Bakke switches back and forth between electricity and heat generation, generating either between 0 to 63 megawatts of electricity or 157 to 247 megawatts of district heating.

Each year, some 100,000 pounds (45,000 kilograms) of ash collected from the waste-incineration process will be reused to build roads, and some 90 percent of the metals in the waste stream will be salvaged. The plant also collects 264,000 gallons (1 million liters) of water through flue gas condensation, which is purified and released through a tall exhaust pipe at its pinnacle. The pipe was not only designed to be a functional exhaust but also offer a wow-factor element: it was originally conceived to blow steam rings, but it now just releases a steady stream.

Two ski lifts take visitors up to the 328-foot-tall (100 meter) slope, which allows for all types of skiing—freestyle and slalom—along with snowblading and snowboarding. On the Amager Bakke website, one can reserve a time to snow plow down the bunny hill or race down the steepest slope at US$20 an hour. Visitors can also rent equipment, take a ski class, or join SKI365, the building's ski club. Because the slope is built using specialized artificial turf, people will be able to ski up there year-round.

It is clear from their website that the five municipalities that own the Amager Resource Center (ARC), the joint municipal company behind Amager Bakke, have tried to design the space for everyone: "If you're a beginner, a shark on skis, freestyler, casual skier, man, woman, boy, girl, thick, thin, tall, or short, then you are part of the community. We have something for everyone. There are red-black, blue, and green courses. In addition, there is also a slalom course, freestyle park, and, of course, an area for kids."

For those who don't ski, there are freely accessible paths sloping up a 5 to 35 percent grade, which one can walk up or go for a heart-pounding run on. Landscape architects with SLA planted more than 130 trees and hundreds of pollinator-friendly bushes and shrubs in social spaces. Amid the social spaces, Amager Bakke invites you to "take a picnic in the shrubbery or just enjoy the view on one of the reclining benches." There's also a club for trail-running enthusiasts, RUN365, with CrossFit-training options for members.

The facility replaced an older coal-incineration plant. The cost of building Amager Bakke was shared among the five municipalities that formed ARC in order to sell the facility's heat and power. But according to *Bloomberg*, the city government thinks it could be the tourism money, rather than the heat or power, that will end up offsetting the largest share of the cost. Only a 13-minute drive from the Copenhagen airport, it will be hard for first-time visitors—particularly those with kids—to avoid making a stop.

In a press briefing, Ingels said, "CopenHill is so clean that we have been able to turn its building mass into the bedrock of the social life of the city: its facade is climbable, its roof is hike-able, and its slopes are skiable. This is a crystal-clear example of hedonistic sustainability: that a sustainable city is not only better for the environment but also more enjoyable for the lives of its citizens."

*Parts of this text reprinted with the permission of the American Society of Landscape Architects (ASLA).*

OPPOSITE **Landscape architecture firm SLA made the public-facing side of Amager Bakke more inviting through the addition of trees and grasses. The building's facade is made of 3.9-by-10.8-foot-wide (1.2-by-3.3-meter) aluminum bricks alternating with glazed windows that bring light to the interior administrative offices.**

TOP **Astroturf covers the 2,000-foot-long (609 meter) slope, which makes it fun for skiers and snowboarders year-round. Walking and running trails separated from the slopes by grasses and shrubs provide more options to enjoy the facility. There are also elevators that take visitors to open spaces near the top, so everyone has the chance to see the views.**

BOTTOM **There are green, blue, and red-black slopes, and even an area set up for slalom races. Skiers sit on sleek lifts that carry them back up the hill after their run.**

RIGHT **Landscape architects at SLA planted 130 trees, hundreds of pollinator-friendly shrubs and bushes, and grasses to create a natural mountain environment amid the infrastructure. The firm says Amager Bakke is designed to be a "green bomb" that will spread seeds to the areas surrounding the power plant.**

LEFT **This view could be from a real hill, except perhaps for the steam being exhausted from the vents. Visitors who reach near the top of Amager Bakke are rewarded with expansive views of the Öresund, the strait that separates Denmark from Sweden, and Middelgrunden, an offshore wind farm that generates 40 megawatts of electricity per year.**

OPPOSITE **The interior, which could be mistaken for the inside of a Star Destroyer, includes 10 floors of administrative offices for Amager Resource Center, which manages the power plant. There are also conference rooms and an education center to teach the public about sustainability. On the exterior trails and slopes, visitors can peek in through windows to see the elaborate systems within.**

# Electric Vehicle Charging Station

Fredericia, Denmark

**There are approximately 1 billion** cars on the road, but, in 2019, only an estimated 7 million of those were EVs. Governments have increased support for EVs to reduce the dangerous effects of air pollution in recent years, and carmakers continue to innovate to reduce costs. As a result, in 2017, EV sales hit 1 million worldwide for the first time. Bloomberg New Energy Finance expects sales of EVs to further increase to 11 million by 2025, 30 million by 2030, and then double again to 60 million by 2040, at which time they will account for half of the global auto market. Europe is expected to lead the way in EV sales, accounting for more than 44 percent of the market in the coming decade, followed by China, then the US.

In 2016, carmakers Daimler, BMW, Volkswagen, and Ford formed a joint venture called IONITY and announced plans to build electric "superhighways" across Europe that will offer EV owners access to four hundred high-speed EV-charging stations. Depending on the size of a car's battery and the speed of the charger, an EV can take anywhere from one to ten hours to fully charge.

With "super-high-speed" 360-kilowatt EV chargers that have just been released, charging could be accomplished in as little as eight minutes.

Partnering with Clever, a Danish electric-mobility provider, and E.On, a European electric utility, the Danish architecture firm COBE created a charging station with four high-speed 150-kilowatt chargers, which will eventually be replaced with super-high-speed chargers on the E20 motorway passing through Fredericia, a city in the southeast of Denmark's Jutland peninsula. The charging station is the first of 48 planned on Scandinavian highways and will become part of the broader network of four hundred stations planned as part of the broader European electric superhighway.

COBE comments that "in our busy lives, every minute counts. Charging stations should not only optimize the car's charging time but also offer a meaningful mental break for people to rejuvenate themselves while on the move." Instead of gasoline fumes, exhaust, and dodgy gas station food, COBE offers a comparatively Zen-like experience. Modeling their station after a grove of trees, they constructed modular structures made of certified sustainable woods that provide shade and shelter and are easy to scale up or down based on the number of chargers needed and the size of the lot.

Their first station in Fredericia consists of 12 treelike structures, totaling 4,300 square feet (400 square meters). Underneath, the high-speed chargers can juice up an EV with a 248-mile-range (400 kilometer) battery in 20 to 30 minutes. Once the 360-kilowatt chargers are released, they will be swapped in, further reducing the time needed to charge. The chargers are powered by Denmark's solar and wind energy.

COBE worked with the Danish Society for Nature Conservation to plant diverse native tree, shrub, and grass species to enhance biodiversity in the motorway environment. Nature is perhaps at the core of the station's experience, reinforcing the message that EVs, while seemingly detached from nature, actually better support environmental and human health than fossil-fuel-powered vehicles.

**The EV charging station offers high-speed chargers that can power up EVs in 20 to 30 minutes and a place to relax on the side of the motorway.**

LEFT **COBE** designed the EV charging station to be a modular, scalable "grove" that can expandor contract with different numbers of chargers and locations. Each "tree" consists of a structure made of sustainable, certified woods. Gaps in the trees bring air and light to motorists and the interior landscape of native trees and plants.

OPPOSITE **COBE** hung swings from the wood frame of the station, adding an element of play to the usually dull experience of charging an EV.

POWER COMMUNITY SPACES

OPPOSITE  The center of the station's interior offers a moment of contemplation among native trees and plants, the opposite of the typical gas station.

RIGHT  The station has four high-speed chargers that are a result of a partnership between Danish e-mobility company Clever, gas station company YX, and European utility E.On's energy infrastructure. The chargers are accessible to Clever's subscribers who pay a monthly fee between €35 (US$40) and €78 (US$90), depending on the type of vehicle, for a home charger and unlimited access to public charging stations.

# Hangzhou Inventronics
# Electric Vehicle Charging Station
Hangzhou, China

GLA-Design created a publicly accessible EV-charging station powered by rooftop PV panels at the base of Hangzhou Inventronics headquarters.

**Hangzhou, the capital city of Zhejiang** Province in East China, with a population of nearly 10 million, is known as a high-tech hub. Home of Alibaba, the Chinese e-commerce giant, the ancient city has also been an innovator in another form of technology: clean transportation systems, including electric, plug-in hybrid, and fuel-cell cars and buses; bike and EV shares; and EV charging stations.

Hangzhou was featured in the 2015 Chinese documentary *Under the Dome*, which was viewed over 100 million times in just a few days in China. Formatted after Al Gore's *An Inconvenient Truth* (2006) but with a slew of Chinese environmental statistics, the documentary stated that in 2013, Hangzhou had two hundred days of smog, in large part because the city held the highest number of cars per person in China—one car for every two people.

Hangzhou has made the transition to zero- or low-emission vehicles a priority in order to dramatically reduce the dangerous particulate matter spewing from fossil fuel–powered vehicles, a problem compounded by the lower-cost but higher-emission fuels used by many Chinese drivers. Some 350,000 to 500,000 Chinese are estimated to die from poor air quality each year.

Hangzhou has attacked its car-induced smog problems by building a citywide public-transportation system, with rapid bus service and bus lanes directed to the city center, and by expanding its bike-share system— by 2017, 10 different companies had put an estimated 882,000 shared bikes on the roads.

The city has also rapidly expanded the use of electric, plug-in, and fuel-cell vehicles. According to the International Council on Clean Transportation, Hangzhou has become one of the "20 electric vehicle capitals of the world." These capital cities together accounted for more than 43 percent of the 2 million EVs sold worldwide in 2016, even though they only make up 3 percent of the world's population. Hangzhou purchased thousands of electric buses; created an electric-car-share program; implemented EV-friendly building and parking codes; gave privileged street access to EVs; and instituted an innovative battery swapping system for its fleet of electric taxis, which allows one taxi to travel for 143 miles (230 kilometers) on two or three charged batteries every day.

In addition to benefiting from the Chinese national government's use of subsidies for EVs (up to nearly US$10,000 in the past few years), the city implemented a stringent citywide quota system that made purchasing a car that runs on fossil fuels nearly impossible, while putting low-emission vehicles in reach. The city has also invested in expanding its EV-charging infrastructure, with the goal of having charging stations accessible within 0.6 miles (1 kilometer) or less for everyone by 2020.

At the base of the headquarters of Hangzhou Inventronics, a leading manufacturer of LED-light drivers, architecture firm GLA Design created a striking 1,600-square-foot (150-square-meter) publicly accessible, prefabricated charging station in 2017 that pilots a modular approach used for conventional gas stations. The goal is to reduce costs and make charging stations easily replicable.

Solar panels on the roof of the charging station help power 18 charging stations for vehicles and four for buses. A built-in battery stores energy generated by the panels for use at night. Inspired by Inventronics's work with LEDs, the station also features eye-catching columns and rows of LED lights.

*China Daily* reports that EVs in Hangzhou have eliminated 15,000 tons of fuel consumption and 34,000 tons of greenhouse gas emissions in the city. China is currently leading the world in EVs, thanks to the models established by cities like Hangzhou. China's stated goal is for 60 percent of all vehicles to be electric by 2035.

LEFT **The charging station is easily accessible to vehicle drivers on Jiang Hong road in the Binjiang district of Hangzhou.**

OPPOSITE TOP **An array of PV panels on the roof powers the LEDs and EV-charging systems. A built-in battery stores energy for use in the evening.**

OPPOSITE BOTTOM LEFT **The prefabricated, modular charging station was built in a factory and assembled on-site.**

OPPOSITE BOTTOM RIGHT **Given Hangzhou Inventronics is a LED-light-driver manufacturer, GLA-Design incorporated striking LED light bands amid the aluminum plastic composite panels, which also makes the station accessible at night. The architects ensured that "electricity is the major visual language" of the project.**

HANGZHOU INVENTRONICS ELECTRIC VEHICLE CHARGING STATION

# The National Stadium
Kaohsiung, Taiwan

ABOVE **The dragon form of the National Stadium in Kaohsiung, Taiwan's second largest city, is covered in 8,400 solar panels. The stadium is set within a public park and within walking distance of a Mass Rapid Transit station.**

**Built for the 2009 World Games,** the National Stadium in Kaohsiung, Taiwan, looks like a coiled dragon. But in this case, the dragon's scales are made up of 8,800 solar panels with a 1.14-megawatt-hour capacity, preventing 660 tons of carbon dioxide from entering the atmosphere each year.

Pritzker Architecture Prize–winning Japanese architect Toyo Ito partnered with designers and engineers at the Takenaka Corporation and Fu Tsu Construction Company to create the 116-foot-tall (35.5 meter), 275,000-square-foot (25,550-square-meter) stadium that can seat up to 55,000 spectators.

Ito designed an extra-wide entrance to both generate excitement for visitors arriving to games and to create a sense of openness for the members of the public who use the front square and sports fields even when no sporting events are planned. Formal sporting events at the stadium are now primarily matches between Taiwanese soccer and rugby teams.

The stadium's roof is held up by 32 helical "oscillating hoop spirals" integrated with 159 trusses. The roof structure itself is made up of a "spiral continuum" that safely holds in place thousands of planar solar panels, which range in width from 8 feet (2.4 meters) to 11.4 feet (3.5 meters). The overall form of the stadium "embodies fluid dynamic movement like a vibrant body." This metal dragon looks like it could stir at any moment.

When the stadium isn't in use, energy produced by the solar panels is fed back to Kaohsiung's energy grid. Ito's firm states that the solar power generated by the stadium offsets some 660 tons of greenhouse gas emissions annually. To further reduce its environmental impact, the stadium is set in a lush public park that is walking distance to and from a Mass Rapid Transit station, which dramatically reduces the number of visitors driving to events and contributing to transportation-related greenhouse gas emissions.

LEFT  **The stadium was designed for the 2009 World Games and can seat up to 55,000 spectators.**

RIGHT  **Solar panels are organized into a "spiral continuum" that breathes life into the stadium's form.**

Chapter Three
# POWER EDUCATION

**Power Education**

—

**Schools and Universities**

Schools and universities around the world are becoming increasingly responsive to demands from students and parents for climate action. Educational institutions serving all age groups are incorporating more courses about climate change, ecology, and sustainability into their curricula. Higher education is creating degree programs that empower students who seek to make a positive impact on the environment through access to well-paying green jobs.

These institutions are also using their own buildings and landscapes to educate students, faculty, staff, parents, and the community about the many benefits of integrating renewable energy. Campuses and educational buildings are being reimagined as healthy, inclusive, energy-positive environmental learning centers.

By pushing the boundaries of sustainable design, schools and universities have raised the bar for what can be accomplished in other building sectors. These projects demonstrate how crucial innovation, research, and education are to finding new solutions to the climate crisis.

Power Education demonstrates that leading-edge schools and universities are meeting or exceeding their own energy needs by designing renewable power. Plus many are storing carbon in their wood structures, offsetting emissions from other materials used in the buildings. These institutions show us that these buildings can exist in any climate, for any kind of community.

In Lavale, India, the Avasara Academy, which provides scholarships to underprivileged Indian girls, demonstrates that nearly net-zero energy design doesn't have to be expensive. Harnessing the thermodynamics of hot and cool air, the building uses a "solar chimney" to cool classrooms and dormitories in the tropics. Likewise, the

School of Design and Environment (SDE4) at the National University in Singapore shows that age-old vernacular architectural styles can be modernized to achieve the highest levels of energy performance while also providing comfort in a hot climate.

The School in Port, Switzerland, a kindergarten and elementary school, incorporates rooftop photovoltaic (PV) panels that power the school plus 50 surrounding homes. Its positive energy contribution radiates outward into the community.

The Centre for Interactive Research on Sustainability (CIRS) at the University of British Columbia in Vancouver, Canada, similarly spreads good energy by being a laboratory for automated green building technologies and disseminating knowledge through the release of open-source data. Through their use of structural wood, which stores carbon, both the School in Port and CIRS significantly offset the embodied carbon of other carbon-intensive materials, like concrete and steel.

Lastly, Solar Strand at the University at Buffalo, New York, creates a gateway for the science-focused university, setting a quarter-mile-long PV array in the form of a DNA strand in restored grasses and wetlands. The message of the project is that we can unite renewable energy and ecological restoration, creating a new kind of sustainable landscape.

# Centre for Interactive Research on Sustainability at the University of British Columbia

Vancouver, British Columbia, Canada

**When Professor John Robinson** was director of the Centre for Interactive Research on Sustainability (CIRS) at the University of British Columbia (UBC) in Vancouver, British Columbia, he envisioned a new center that would be at "the front edge of sustainable performance." He imagined a model carbon- and energy-positive building that would house UBC's sustainability experts and also be an integral part of the university's "research infrastructure," a testing ground for new building materials and technologies.

For Robinson, who was the lead author of a number of key reports by the Intergovernmental Panel on Climate Change, which shared the Nobel Peace Prize with former US vice president Al Gore in 2007, another key goal was to "live within the building footprint as much as possible," with the aim of being close to self-sufficient. The vision was realized in 2011 with the opening of a new C$36 million (US$30 million) center that is largely automated through a system of sensors and controls, incorporates creative energy and water-saving measures, and is built primarily with wood.

Architects at Perkins and Will, along with landscape architects at PWL Partnership, engineers at Stantec, and a team of other consultants designed the four-story, 61,000-square-foot (5,668-square-meter) U-shaped building with two wings that wrap around a central atrium, which actually functions as green roof of the auditorium. Windows along the narrow wings, which are just 30 feet (10 meters) wide, ensure that all two hundred researchers and staff inside have access to bright daylight even on cloudy days.

To maintain light but reduce unwanted solar heat gain and cooling energy use, Perkins and Will focused on the windows, reducing their collective area so they account for 30 percent of the facade and using triple-glazed windows on the ground floor and double-glazed windows on the upper levels.

The designers also incorporated multipurpose shading structures over windows. Many of the windows are shaded with PV panels that have a 25-kilowatt capacity, which can meet about 10 percent of the building's power budget. Windows on the western side of the atrium are shaded with a living wall, which also supports employee health and well-being. In the spring and summer, chocolate vines grow in, creating shade; in the fall and winter, the vines wither, letting in sun when the interior most needs warmth. Windows were also designed to be operable, allowing researchers and staff flexibility in cooling or warming their own spaces.

The CIRS leverages renewable sources to heat and cool itself: 40 kilowatts of energy come from evacuated tube solar collectors that preheat water; waste heat is captured from the Earth and Ocean Sciences building next door; and heating and cooling is provided through a geothermal system that exchanges energy with the ground. These systems return 600 megawatt hours back to the UBC's energy grid, preventing some 150 tons of greenhouse gas emissions annually.

The CIRS is not only operationally net-positive in terms of energy and carbon but also structurally carbon positive. Given that the CIRS is made primarily from various types of structural wood, including glulam, FSC-certified wood, and wood from trees killed by pine beetles, the building stores approximately 900 tons of carbon in its structure, more than offsetting the carbon generated through its construction. The CIRS meets all its own water needs as well. The roof collects rainwater that is cleansed for potable use. Wastewater is collected

OPPOSITE **The Centre for Interactive Research on Sustainability was designed to be the most sustainable building in North America. Metal screens across the windows host a green wall where chocolate vines grow. In the summer, they fill in, blocking the sun, which helps to cool the interior; in the winter, they wither, letting in more light to warm the space.**

through a solar aquatics biofiltration system and reused to irrigate the landscape.

The UBC envisioned the CIRS to be a living laboratory. Embedded sensors and controls make up an automated building-performance system, yielding about three thousand data points for researchers. Research conducted on the building's performance to date is available for free on the CIRS website, part of the UBC's commendable effort to be transparent and share both data and lessons learned.

The project is also an experiment in designing and constructing contemporary buildings for longevity. Instead of building the center to last 40 years, the average lifespan of many new buildings, the university asked that the CIRS be built to last a century in order to improve its sustainability. Building systems were designed to be replaceable, so that future researchers will be able to swap in new, better materials and technologies and continue testing into the twenty-second century.

**The U-shaped building ensures that all researchers and staff have access to daylight. The building wraps around an auditorium that is covered in a green roof, which captures stormwater runoff. Recycled wastewater is also used to irrigate the landscape.**

Rows of fixed sunshades integrated with PV panels not only reduce solar heat gain within interior spaces but also have a 25-kilowatt capacity, which can meet 10 percent of the building's annual energy use.

# Solar Strand, University at Buffalo

Buffalo, New York, United States

Solar Strand is made up of
3,200 PV panels arranged
in the form of a DNA strand.
Landscape designer Walter
Hood explained: "You read
these little blips in DNA, which
are codified through a linear
script." Hood Design Studio
wrote a programming script
to organize the panels.

In 2007, the University at Buffalo (UB) formed an ambitious plan to become carbon neutral by 2030. Two years later, the New York Power Authority (NYPA) approached the UB about creating a solar power plant on its campus. The NYPA proposed a power facility segregated from the community by a chain-link fence; the university, instead, came back with the idea of a highly visible, beautiful 15-acre (6-hectare) solar power installation integrated into campus life. In partnership with the NYPA, the university initiated a design competition for the $7.5 million project. The landscape architecture and urban design firm Hood Design Studio won with its Solar Strand design.

A quarter-mile-long (0.4 kilometer) array of PV panels now forms a dramatic gateway to the north campus. Its 750-kilowatt capacity powers seven hundred on-campus apartments. The project saves an estimated $100,000 in electricity costs and means 400 fewer tons of greenhouse gas emissions enter the atmosphere each year.

Walter Hood, a public artist, landscape designer, and professor at the University of California at Berkeley, sought to integrate scientific ideas into the design of the array in order to highlight the UB's role as a major public research university. During a Zoom interview, Hood explained: "Through our observations, we came upon the idea of a DNA strand that runs parallel along right edges. This linear landscape form was a way to organize the PV panels and address ecology. The university wanted Solar Strand to be a new gateway to the north campus and create a new identity, so we took 3,200 PV panels and organized them into a 140-foot-wide (42 meter), 1,250-foot-long (380 meter) DNA-strand formation."

Hood designed the strand to be highly visible and flank visitors as they enter the north campus. The design sends a clear signal about the increasingly important role science and renewable energy infrastructure must play in our society.

Another goal was to make the space accessible and educational, a place to teach UB students, members of the community, and local elementary, middle, and high school students about renewable energy and sustainability. Amid the panels, multiple outdoor classrooms are paved with one thousand tons of bricks and concrete slabs recycled from campus buildings and landscapes. Paths and classroom spaces enable visitors to get up close to the panels, which vary in height from 4 to 28 feet (1.2 to 8.5 meters).

In an interview with *Domus*, Walter G. Shibley, professor and dean of the UB's School of Architecture and Planning, said,

The lowest-level bracket is set at the height of a human being, about 4 feet. You can see over and around it. As you move through the double and triple stacks, there's a rhythm in the landscape. From the inside, one is always grounded in multiple views and perceptions.

From the outside, you don't see a monolith, but staggered heights, scaling up and down. Also, what might seem purely a technical function—two steel pipes that run the length of the strand to enclose a vast network of wiring—is also a human element, as visitors have come to use these as seats or foot rests. In some spots, the steel piping is set back so visitors can get up close and touch the panels.

As part of the planning phase, Hood's firm researched the history of the campus and site and discovered a creek that runs through the campus had been moved during campus development. Part of the Solar Strand site is in the old watershed of that creek, so Hood and his team also saw the project as an opportunity for ecological preservation and restoration. To reinforce the sense that renewable energy creates a positive ripple effect through the environment, the team restored expansive meadows and indigenous vernal pools surrounding the installation. University faculty, student, and staff volunteers planted trees throughout the site. The comprehensive ecological-restoration effort helped bring wildlife back to the area. Through landscape design, renewable energy and nature form a new harmony.

*Parts of this text reprinted with the permission of the American Society of Landscape Architects (ASLA).*

During its opening to the Buffalo community on Earth Day in 2014, university students, faculty, staff, and the surrounding community mingled in the outdoor classrooms set within the strand formation.

LEFT **Local K–12 students come to Solar Strand to learn about renewable energy and sustainability. The brackets holding up the PV panels range in height from 4 to 28 feet. To make the space safe for the public, electrical wiring for the PV panels was encased in steel pipes that run the length of the installation on either side of the pathway. The steel pipes were also designed to work as seats or footrests.**

BELOW **Even elementary-school children have the opportunity to learn about the importance of renewable energy.**

Solar Strand is also an ecological-restoration project. Hood and the university let the native meadow landscape around Solar Strand grow in and enabled ecological succession through seasonal mowing. Hood says: "Where the university mowed, wildflowers came in. This beautiful place went through change." As diversity within the landscape increased, university staff started to spot animals. Hood told the university "that is the kind of environment you want here."

ABOVE Hood finds that "the most powerful image of Solar Strand is in the winter when you see the snow dripping off the PV panels." He discovered that "solar energy can be used in places you never thought possible."

LEFT Pathways from nearby campus roads take visitors through meadows to Solar Strand. The landscape design reinforces the connection between ecology and renewable energy.

# School in Port
Port, Switzerland

The School in Port, designed by **Skop Architects, is one of the most sustainable and healthy schools in the world.**

In northwest Switzerland, Port, a small suburb of the city of Biel, has a population of 3,500. Settled for more than six thousand years by Neolithic, Viking, Roman, and now Swiss communities, it is home to one of the most sustainable, healthy, and inventive educational facilities in the world— a kindergarten and elementary school built primarily of wood that generates enough power not only for itself but also 50 surrounding homes.

Zurich-based Skop Architects, which was founded by partners Martin Zimmerli, Silvia Weibel Hendriksen, and Basil Spiess, won a competition in 2013 to design the energy-positive school for 280 children. And in 2017, the environmentally and socially responsible community hub came to fruition.

The jagged forms of the school's wood roof are inspired by the pitched roofs of typical houses in Port and by the forms of the surrounding Jura Mountains. They hold 1,100 PV panels that have the capacity to generate nearly 300 kilowatts of power at peak times. Wood-casing elements in the roof structure bear the load of the roof panels, which can span 42 feet (13 meters). Cavities within the casings enable air transfer from room to room for the ventilation system and contain insulation that dampens noise.

Skop Architects worked with timber engineers Indermühle Bauingenieure to ensure that the principally wood structures could support the two-story 26,600-square-foot (2,470-square-meter) building and rooftop panels. Some 507 prefabricated wood elements were carefully joined on-site. Wood is used throughout the school as the primary construction material, as Zimmerli describes: "Wood, which is the only construction material that stores carbon, is used throughout both the facade and the interior, in fact, all the way down to the furniture. As a result, the school can be seen as a large carbon sink. And all the timber comes from sustainable forestry."

The first story of the school is reserved for faculty spaces, including recreation, administrative, and conference rooms. The upper story is separated into an elementary school and kindergarten. The elementary school has nine classrooms that connect to common workshop and multipurpose rooms. The kindergarten, made up of three classrooms, painting studios, and other shared spaces, is separated from the rest of the elementary school.

"Classrooms offer direct access to group working spaces and a generous multifunctional middle zone," notes architect Spiess, "which allows maximum flexibility for current and future teaching and learning methodologies. Large parts of the interior walls are also floor-to-ceiling magnetic blackboards, which invite students to express themselves." In the era of COVID-19, these flexible spaces also enable administrators to spread out students, as needed, for social-distancing purposes.

The classrooms benefit from natural light pouring through seven skylights and large windows that offer views of the surrounding green play spaces. Numerous scientific studies have shown that views of nature and access to daylight significantly increase students' cognition and ability to recover from stress, thereby improving learning outcomes.

For Weibel Hendriksen, the classrooms also create an important feeling of safety. They "naturally benefit from the spatial qualities of the folded roof. Each classroom appears to be an independent little house, creating a cozy and homelike atmosphere for the children."

During the cold Swiss winters, the building is heated by waste from an incineration plant in Biel. But the airtight building envelope and continuous renewal of air in the building through a ventilation system also helps ensure that the educational spaces are not only comfortable but also energy efficient. Operable windows allow the school's administrators flexibility to take advantage of natural cross ventilation in warmer months. The continuous renewal of air and operable windows also helps reduce the risk of exposure to airborne viruses.

OPPOSITE **The kindergarten classrooms offer large windows with access to daylight from two directions. The windows offer views of surrounding green play spaces, which improve the cognition, mood, and stress reduction abilities of the students.**

RIGHT **Multifunctional hallways form a middle zone between classrooms, and workshop spaces have floor-to-ceiling magnetic blackboards that enable children to express themselves. Windows near the ceiling allow daylight to pour in.**

LEFT **Amid views of the trees, sports fields, and surrounding hills, one of the playgrounds around the school offers neighborhood children who bike to school a covered bicycle-parking area.**

OPPOSITE **The jagged roof of the School in Port is covered in 1,100 PV panels that generate nearly 300 kilowatts of energy, enough to power both the school and 50 surrounding homes. Seven skylights allow sunlight to pour into the classrooms and common spaces.**

# Avasara Academy
Lavale, India

LEFT  **Nearly 300 disadvantaged young women from Western India study leadership and entrepreneurship at the nearly net-zero energy Avasara Academy. The patio in the foreground is made from waste materials from local quarries and product manufacturers. The building facade is covered in bamboo shade screens handmade by local artisans.**

OPPOSITE  **Avasara Academy shows how waste materials can be beautiful. Outdoor mosaic-paved areas were "meticulously crafted from marble and limestone sourced from the waste material generated in factories, shops, and quarries." Case Design states they are "available at a fraction of the cost and more durable than industrially produced options."**

**Roopa Purushothaman was determined** to create a secondary school that could lift up disadvantaged young women from Western India and give them the skills to become the future leaders of India and the world. After forming the Avasara Leadership Institute, a nonprofit organization, in 2011, she partnered with architect Samuel Barclay, founder of India-based Case Design, two years later to build an equally forward-thinking campus for her school: Avasara Academy, an expansive sustainable educational hub, where hundreds of young women now live and learn, in the valley of Lavale, near Pune.

Using smart, low-tech strategies complemented by arrays of rooftop PV panels, Avasara Academy is working toward net-zero energy use while creating a "sanctuary for learning," a place where Muslim, Hindu, and Christian teachers instruct students in the values of "integrity, reflection, excellence, empathy, interdependence, fortitude, and optimism." Approximately 275 young women, aged 12 to 18, study on the campus, which is designed to eventually expand to accommodate up to six hundred students. Students pay about 5 percent of fees, while donors in India and the US finance the rest. The curriculum is focused on leadership and social entrepreneurship.

On a 182,000-square-foot (17,000-square-meter) site, the school buildings take up 152,000 square feet (14,120 square meters). According to Barclay, principal architect of the campus, a decision was made early on to build a number of smaller buildings that create a "more intimate and domestic scale" for the young women living away from home for the first time. Each building has classrooms on the ground and first floors, organized by subject, while the upper levels house dormitories, ensuring that each building is used day and night.

Case Design worked with Pratik Raval, an engineer with Transsolar KlimaEngineering, to devise an innovative system that uses daily temperature changes to cool the spaces, eliminating the need for mechanical systems and saving the school money in the process. Through digital modeling, the team was able to design a system that includes solar chimneys; earth ducts; windows with shade structures; and floors and ceilings that use thermal-massing strategies to absorb and store heat during the day—all of which improve the health and comfort of the students and teachers year-round.

Each building has a series of solar chimneys, which are central, vertical open spaces running from the foundation to the roof and which use convection to draw in cool air through a set of horizontal concrete earth ducts buried in the structure foundations. The ducts open on the north facade of each building and are kept cool through shading from the building, trees, and plants. Air traveling through the ducts is then further cooled by the lower ambient air temperatures in the building foundations. This continuous air flow pulled in through the ducts and windows circulates up through the classrooms and dormitories. Each room has ceiling fans that help mix in incoming cool air before the rising warmer air exits into the ceiling vents, which exhaust through the solar chimneys on the rooftop.

"By studying the building and material physics of each structure," stated Barclay, "it became clear that the thermal mass of the ceiling and floor concrete structures would help cool the internal spaces. For this reason, there are no false ceilings or floor coverings." Deep verandas, overhangs, and bamboo screens handcrafted by local artisans were also incorporated to further reduce the impact of the strong Indian sun.

Another benefit of Avasara Academy's approach to cooling and ventilation, which enables continuous airflow, is that it creates a healthier environment for students and teachers. As Barclay describes it: "I am confident the earth ducts and solar chimneys help reduce the spread of germs and bacteria. Most conventional mechanical systems have filters to deal with stale and recirculating air. Our system provides a constant supply of fresh air brought in from the outside."

Each of the six planned buildings will be topped with an array of PV panels. As of mid-2018, the first two buildings created on campus produced enough energy to meet 85 percent of their energy needs, with excess energy sent to the local grid during peak sun hours.

Case Design incorporated recycled and reused materials to reduce the greenhouse gas emissions from the construction of the school and also to support the thermal massing of the spaces. Main partition walls are made of bricks constructed of fly ash, a coal-production waste product, made locally in Pune. Local artisans hand-formed shards of colorful stones and waste from local quarries and other local material producers into colorful mosaic floors that contribute to the thermal massing. According to Barclay, the sustainability features of their academy have been integrated into the curriculum: "The young women have become passionate about it; the reclaimed and recycled materials are especially popular."

LEFT **Local artisans mix indigo pigments and dyes to make the indigo paint used to coat Avasara Academy's ceilings.**

OPPOSITE **Danish artist Malene Bach and local artisans used local pigments and dyes to create an indigo paint to cover the concrete ceilings, which are exposed to support the air flow generated by ceiling windows and fans and the thermal massing of the structures.**

LEFT  **The concrete-earth ducts installed in the foundation of each of the campus buildings were locally constructed.**

RIGHT  **A diagram of the smart, low-tech natural cooling system in Avasara Academy's buildings. The solar chimney, in the center of the building, draws in cool, moist air (depicted in blue) from the earth ducts and windows and exhausts warmer air (depicted in red) out the roof. The system was developed through collaboration between Case Design and Pratik Raval from Transsolar KlimaEngineering.**

OPPOSITE  **Ceiling vents behind screens, above the bookshelves in this image, pull warmer air into the central solar chimney. Locally sourced marble and limestone, which were deemed cheaper and more durable than wood, were used to create shelves. Recycled colored glass was incorporated into the terrazzo table.**

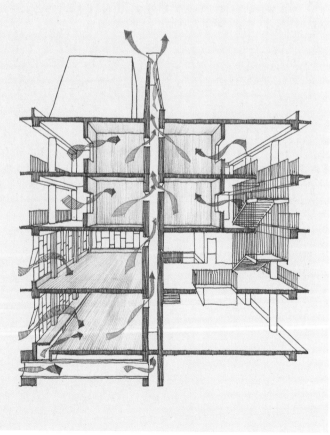

# SDE4 at the National University of Singapore
Singapore

Inspired by Indigenous Malay houses, SDE4 uses a dramatic over-sailing roof to reduce the impact of sunlight on learning spaces and create a platform for 1,225 PV panels that generate 500 megawatt hours of electricity annually.

**For the 50th anniversary, in 2019,** of the School of Design and Environment (SDE) at the National University of Singapore, the university planned something special: SDE4, Singapore's first net-zero energy building. Designed by Serie Architects and Multiply Architects, along with Surbana Jurong, the 92,440-square-foot (8,588-square-meter) six-story building shows how net-zero energy can be achieved in the tropics through the use of vernacular approaches.

The building is inspired by the indigenous simple timber Malay houses of the region, which are characterized by deep overhangs, raised platforms, and loose room divisions that enable continuous cross ventilation. According to Christopher Lee, cofounder and principal of Serie Architects, the team designed a contemporary version of the Malay roof for SDE4 not only to protect against the tropical sun but also as a surface for the 1,225 PV panels that power the building. The panels have an annual energy generating capacity of 500 megawatt hours.

Beneath the dramatic canopy, the architects purposefully blurred the boundaries between inside and outside. More than 50 percent of the building—including common areas, circulation corridors, and stairwells—is open to the surrounding campus and naturally ventilated. Most of the learning spaces can also be opened to the prevailing winds. This enables a significant reduction in energy use for air conditioning. As Lee describes: "One of our ambitions when we started the project was to challenge the notion that a highly energy-efficient building had to be opaque. We envisioned a very transparent volume in which the outside and inside spaces are ambiguous; where nature and landscape play an important part."

The southern side of the overhanging roof forms a tropical portico over mature trees the design team preserved. This brings the landscape up close to the buildings' classrooms, creating an immersive sense of nature within the learning spaces. The east and west facades are designed as "veils," with aluminum curtains that filter out strong sunlight but preserve views. As four hundred students, faculty, and staff travel through the building, they are continuously exposed to daylight and shifting views of the campus forest.

The design team imagined the building as a series of platforms that break down barriers between research, design, and learning. On the six levels, there are 16,415 square feet (1,525 square meters) of studio design space, a 5,380-square-foot (500-square-meter) open plaza, a variety of public and social spaces, workshop and research centers, and a café and library. These spaces flow into each other and into terraces and landscaped balconies in order to encourage chance encounters, socializing, and collaboration. According to Lee, "There are no formal boundaries between places to work, socialize, and study."

Rooms that require a cooler, more comfortable environment for studying and working use a hybrid cooling system designed by Transsolar Klima-Engineering that supplies rooms with "100 percent fresh precooled air, albeit at higher temperatures and humidity levels than in a conventional system." Ceiling fans augment the system and help alleviate any discomfort from the higher temperatures and humidity. The hybrid cooling system reduces energy use for cooling by an estimated 36 to 56 percent over a conventional system.

Singapore, which now calls itself a "city in a garden," aims to become the most sustainable city in the world. These environmental values have taken form in their strong biophilic design culture. In 2009, the RMJM-designed Khoo Teck Puat Hospital, as a reimagined medical facility and a green hub, opened to the community. In 2013, Singapore-based WOHA architects built the PARKROYAL on Pickering as a hotel in a garden. And in 2019, the glass-encased Jewel Changi airport, designed by Safdie Architects and PWP Landscape Architecture, opened with a 6-acre (2.4-hectare) indoor forest of 2,500 trees and 100,000 shrubs. The SDE4 is the latest example of Singapore's bold and increasingly influential approach to designing with nature and technology.

OPPOSITE **More than 50 percent of the interior of SDE4 is open to the surrounding campus environment. Natural ventilation of common areas significantly reduces energy use for cooling. Deep overhangs keep out strong, direct sunlight.**

BOTTOM **A central auditorium is connected to surrounding classrooms and also creates a pathway to lower levels. According to Christopher Lee, a cofounder and principal at Serie Architects, the building flow "purposefully bleeds from one research and learning space to another." The goal is to encourage chance encounters, socializing, and student collaboration around designing and prototyping.**

RIGHT **Design studios were designed to be open, flexible spaces that can be used for multiple purposes. Air conditioning is only used when necessary. Vents along the top of the windows open to allow natural ventilation. When the hybrid cooling system is turned on, ceiling fans circulate the air.**

ABOVE **Under the south side of the roof, landscaped balconies offer impressive views of the lush campus, which is near the southern coastline of Singapore. The design team added layers of biophilic elements to improve health and well-being.**

OPPOSITE **On the east and west facades of SDE4, walls of aluminum "veils" help reduce direct sunlight from hitting interior spaces, which helps further reduce the need for air conditioning.**

Chapter Four
# POWER OFFICES

## Power Offices

—

## Commercial, Governmental, and Institutional Buildings

While teleworking is the most sustainable way to work for those who have the option (and safest in the era of COVID-19), 21st-century business still requires places to meet and work. Office buildings for commercial, governmental, and institutional use can create a sense of community and reduce loneliness, boost engagement and productivity, and spur creativity and innovation.

At their best, communal work spaces can meet their own energy needs by incorporating renewable energy and offsetting or reducing energy use and can also be designed to benefit from the seasonal and diurnal paths of the sun. Work spaces can also lower energy use by incorporating operable windows that enable natural ventilation and mechanical ventilation systems that continuously draw in outside air, thereby eliminating the recirculation of inside air and reducing the risk of exposure to viruses like SARS-CoV-2, which causes COVID-19, and microorganisms. Taking these steps significantly improves employee health, well-being, and satisfaction, which also means increased productivity and less absenteeism.

The operations and construction of commercial buildings account for approximately half of all building greenhouse gas emissions, which make up 40 percent of all emissions. To keep warming below 1.5 degrees Celsius (2.7 degrees Fahrenheit), a key target outlined in the Paris Climate Accord, all existing office buildings need to be retrofitted to achieve net-zero emissions by 2050, and all new office buildings need to be built to achieve the same goal by 2030.

According to groups like Architecture 2030, the World Green Building Council, and Center for Climate and Energy Solutions, there are two major obstacles to meeting these goals: the annual rate of retrofitting isn't nearly high enough and, with population growth, the amount of office space is expected to increase by 40 percent by 2050.

Multiple US states, notably California and New York, the European Union, and many cities worldwide are speeding the transition to net-zero or nearly net-zero energy office buildings with new mandates and incentives for retrofits and new development. Still, many other national and state governments need to join the effort.

Office buildings can go a long way toward meeting their own energy needs and can significantly reduce or eliminate their greenhouse gas emissions by combining a few key approaches:

- Generate renewable energy through rooftop- or facade-photovoltaic (PV) panels or purchase all-renewable energy.
- Go fully electric, eliminating the use of oil and gas for cooling and heating.
- Significantly reduce energy use through efficient heating, cooling, and ventilation systems.
- Incorporate window, shading, and lighting systems designed for the sun's seasonal and diurnal paths.

Office buildings can also be designed and constructed to last longer than the conventional 40-year lifespan and store carbon in their structures, reducing the impact of their embodied carbon and emissions from employees commuting.

Power Offices shows how good design enables these approaches to work together as systems. These buildings combine renewable energy generation with energy efficiency and solar responsiveness to improve employee health and well-being.

The ecologically regenerative Brock Environmental Center in Virginia Beach, Virginia, an office and conference center for the Chesapeake Bay Foundation, demonstrates that a building can meet all its own energy and water needs, be oriented and designed to maximize daylight in work areas, and improve energy efficiency.

Similarly, the David and Lucile Packard Foundation in Los Altos, California, one of the largest net-zero energy buildings in the United States, combines smart orientation and design with overhangs and automated blinds systems to maximize employee health and well-being while reducing solar heat gain, glare, and energy use for air conditioning. The foundation's headquarters also features locally sourced, recycled, and sustainably harvested materials and native plant gardens.

A significant portion of the Bullitt Center in Seattle, Washington, designed with the ambitious goal of being the most sustainable office building in the world, is made of structural timber sustainably harvested from local forests. The six-story building, which is designed to last 250 years, meets all its own energy and water needs and stores 600 tons of carbon dioxide in its frame.

Two projects, Council House 2 and Pearl River Tower, artfully demonstrate how to scale up responsiveness to site and environment. The ten-story Council House 2 in Melbourne, Australia, is a government office building that mimics the mutually supportive and responsive functions of an ecosystem to reduce energy use by 60 percent in comparison with a conventional Australian office building. Its air-conditioning system doesn't recirculate air. Eighty percent of staff working in the building prefer it to their previous office.

The supertall 71-story Pearl River Tower in Guangzhou, China, also lowers energy use by 60 percent in comparison with a typical Chinese skyscraper, largely due to the fact that air is naturally drawn into the floors of each story, filtered, and then circulated. The building is also oriented to maximize natural light and energy production from PV panels and built-in wind turbines.

# The David and Lucile Packard Foundation

Los Altos, California, United States

The David and Lucile Packard Foundation, which was founded in 1964 by David Packard, a cofounder of Hewlett-Packard, and his wife, Lucile, is one of the largest foundations in the US, with assets of $7.6 billion. In 2018, the foundation awarded $332 million in grants to nonprofits in order to "improve the lives of children, enable creative pursuit of science, advance reproductive health, and conserve and restore Earth's natural systems."

In 2006, the foundation initiated the process of fully redesigning its headquarters, located on a triangular 1.8-acre (0.7-hectare) site in the business district of Los Altos, California. The foundation made a conscious decision to live its values and sought a "physical manifestation" of its "long-term commitment to conserving the Earth's natural resources," as well as "a comfortable, healthful space" for its employees to "work collaboratively." The new headquarters would offer "support for a vital downtown in the community that has been the foundation's home for 45 years."

Six years later, a new net-zero 50,000-square-foot (4,645-square-meter) headquarters opened, making it one of the largest energy-self-sufficient office buildings in the US. The $38 million building, which was designed by a team led by San Francisco–based architecture firm EHDD, features two long, narrow two-story wings covered in 915 PV panels that generate 418 megawatt hours of electricity a year. The two wings, which are 250 feet (76 meters) long by 45 feet (13 meters) wide, are parallel; two short perpendicular wings bridge either end, forming a lush interior courtyard.

The building has long parallel wings that maximize the staff's exposure to daylight from both the exterior and the interior courtyard. All this daylight also reduces energy consumption for lighting by 30 percent. Automated systems measure the levels of daylight throughout the day and brighten or dim lights as needed. Additional "light shelves" facing in along the interior of windows further project and reflect natural light into the office spaces. Furthermore, desktop sensors in each workstation automatically turn off lights and computers when any of the foundation's 120 staff members are away from their desks.

EHDD worked with building engineers and energy modelers at Integral Group and daylighting experts at Loisos + Ubbelohde to optimize the daylighting and energy efficiency of the building envelope. Given that it made sense to align the building with Second Street, which angles 40 degrees to the south, one long edge of the building would face the southwest, exposing interior spaces to solar heat gain and glare.

To resolve the issue, EHDD designed deep overhangs over windows along the southwest facade and added shade trees, balconies, and external movable blinds made by Nysan that are programmed to open and close based on the diurnal cycle of the sun. Windows used throughout are "triple element," made of two panels of glazing that sandwich 1.5 inches (3.8 centimeters) of argon gas and a suspended heat mirror film, all of which provides superior insulation for conventional windows.

The headquarters uses a system of air handlers that draw in, filter, and dehumidify air and then blow the air across beams filled with either warmed or chilled water. Simply blowing air against the beams is enough to either warm or cool the spaces. For air conditioning, water is chilled at night by a compressor-free cooling tower and then stored in two 25,000-gallon (94,600-liter) underground tanks before it circulates through the beams. Windows are also operable to enable natural ventilation during temperate weather.

The building facade, which appears to almost glow before sunset, is clad in architectural copper, a mostly recycled material that will develop a nice patina, FSC-certified western red cedar, and stone sourced from Mount Moriah on the border of Utah and Nevada, less than 500 miles (804 kilometers) away.

OPPOSITE **The David and Lucile Packard Foundation is one of the largest net-zero energy office spaces in the US. The facade is clad in architectural copper, western red cedar, and Mount Moriah stone.**

Two long, narrow wings and two shorter perpendicular wings define a central courtyard that brings light and fresh air into the surrounding office space. London Plane trees were selected for their ability to generate shade but not grow tall enough to obstruct the PV panels. The landscape, which is made up of 90 percent native plants, was designed by landscape architects at Joni L. Janecki & Associates to reduce water use and also capture 90 percent of run-off from the building.

BELOW LEFT **EHDD** organized "triple-element" windows into playful and functional patterns. Exterior blinds by Nysan are programmed to open and close based on the diurnal cycle of the sun, reducing solar heat gain in interior spaces as needed. The blinds include just some of the 15,000 monitoring and control points managed through the automated system.

BELOW RIGHT **A glimpse** of the unique internal heating and cooling system. Chilled water is moved through the air-conditioning system using variable speed pumps and pipes angled at 130 degrees, rather than the usual 90 degrees. According to the Packard Foundation, this reduces duct work and pump energy use by 75 percent.

ABOVE **The headquarters**, which provides office space for 120 staff, includes a variety of informal outdoor meeting spaces in the courtyard and on balconies. When weather permits, the Foundation opens the windows and relies on natural ventilation for heating and cooling, further reducing energy use.

# Brock Environmental Center
Virginia Beach, Virginia, United States

LEFT **The Chesapeake Bay Foundation (CBF)'s Brock Environmental Center is energy-positive, producing more energy than it uses; meets its own water needs; and produces no wastewater or sewage. The center serves as the CBF's primary educational hub for teaching thousands of local K–12 students about the need to restore the bay's fragile ecosystems.**

OPPOSITE **The center is set within a 118-acre (47-hectare) public park, an ecologically rich landscape made up of wetlands and meadows that provides habitat for 28 species of birds.**

### The Chesapeake Bay Foundation

(CBF)'s Brock Environmental Center is the result of a successful partnership formed in 2012 between CBF, the City of Virginia Beach, and the Trust for Public Land. These partners came together with the goal of saving 118 acres (47 hectares) of the bay's fragile ecosystem in Virginia Beach's Pleasure House Point from a proposed massive housing development and succeeded in turning the land into a public park.

After the collaboration purchased the land from a private owner, CBF transformed a 10-acre (4-hectare) segment of the land, which was once a brownfield, into a highly sustainable and resilient hub for its offices and public environmental-education programs. The CBF engaged architecture firm SmithGroup and civil, surveying, and landscape architecture firm WPL to design an educational center, where they could teach the public how to restore the bay watershed and landscape.

In 2015, the 10,500-square-foot (975-square-meter) center opened, creating office space for 25 staff—from the CBF and partner organizations—meeting rooms, an 80-seat conference room, and an outdoor classroom, which now hosts thousands of local K–12 students each year. The center is one of the few buildings to meet the stringent guidelines of the Living Building Challenge: it is not only energy-positive, producing more energy than it needs, but also meets its own water needs, produces no wastewater or sewage, and restores the degraded environment.

The Pleasure House Point site is where Pleasure House Creek, Crab Creek, and Western Branch Lynnhaven River meet and flow into the Chesapeake Bay, creating an ecologically rich area. William Almond, a landscape architect and principal at WPL, commented, "Until the 1960s, the land was intertidal marsh, providing valuable habitat for a range of animal and plant life. In the 1970s, the dredging of Lynnhaven Inlet resulted in extensive spoils deposited on-site, significantly damaging wetlands."

This once-degraded landscape is a perfect site for the CBF to educate the public about the bay's complex history of ecological disturbance and the value of restoration and renewal. WPL designed plans for restoring the damaged brownfield site and reestablishing natural wetlands. Through natural succession, former marshes filled with dredge spoils are now transitioning into salt meadows. On the north end of the site, an old-growth maritime forest remains.

SmithGroup optimized the placement and size of windows to maximize daylight and limit solar heat gain. Triple-paned windows make up 25 percent of the building's facade. At top left, clerestory windows on the north side of the building pour light onto work surfaces. At right, a porch overhang along the length of the building's south elevation provides shade that prevents bright light from entering the workspace from the south. Operable windows and ceiling fans help further reduce energy use.

To restore the site and surrounding ecosystem and to prepare for the anticipated rise of sea levels, the design team decided to set the building inland 200 feet (61 meters) from the wetlands, near the edge of the forest, and raise the building 14 feet (4.2 meters) above the existing floodplain. During construction, no trees were destroyed, only relocated, and "aggressive limits of disturbance" were set around the perimeter.

The design team built on this respectful approach to the bay through a range of inventive strategies that reduce the environmental impact of the new center. The building produces 80 percent more energy than it needs each year through a PV array with a 45-kilowatt capacity on its south-facing roof and two 10-kilowatt wind turbines on either end of the site.

The center is oriented along an east–west axis to maximize daylight, thereby reducing the need for lighting energy by 97 percent. To reduce energy spent on cooling, the center supports natural ventilation through operable windows, ceiling fans, and a design that encourages cross ventilation by taking advantage of southwest and northeast winds. According to SmithGroup, "carefully placed and frugally sized" triple-paned windows on the north, south, and east elevations of the building offer daylight and views while limiting solar heat gain. To maximize thermal performance and reduce air infiltration, the firm designed an airtight and insulated building envelope.

The architects incorporated a variable refrigerant flow (VRF) HVAC system connected to 18 ground-source wells. This approach was deemed more energy efficient and cost-effective than a conventional ground source geothermal heating and cooling system. The system also saved the organization from having to purchase an additional $15,000 in PV panels to maintain the goal of achieving net-zero energy.

According to Cindy Cogil, the project's lead mechanical engineer at SmithGroup, the dedicated outdoor air system and VRF HVAC system incorporated into the Brock Environmental Center also provides health benefits in the era of the coronavirus: "We have found research to support that well-ventilated buildings protect occupants from the spread of viruses like SARS-CoV-2 that causes COVID-19." The HVAC system uses a dedicated outside air system that decouples ventilation from heating and cooling. In addition, the center "uses both natural ventilation and night flushing of inside air." The health benefits of natural ventilation are clear: "It not only provides higher degree of air dilution but also generally results in cross flow air patterns that limit mixing and recirculation."

The CBF pays just $17 for a monthly connection fee to the utility and receives a $1,400 annual rebate from them for all the power it sends back to the grid. A survey of employees found that the center accomplishes the energy goals while also exceeding standard benchmarks on lighting, air quality,

and thermal comfort. The center achieves net-zero water use by collecting rainwater from its roofs, filtering and disinfecting it with ozone and UV light, and then using it to fulfill all of its water-supply needs. Two 1,650-gallon (6,240-liter) cisterns enable the center to maintain operation up to six weeks during drought conditions.

Composting toilets eliminate the need for a sewage connection; solid waste is used as compost on-site, and leachate is sent to a local struvite reactor, where it is converted into fertilizer. Greywater from sinks and showers is channeled to a greywater rain garden designed by WPL.

According to Cogil, the composting toilets also provide an added health benefit: they "exhaust air downward, so there is no toilet flush plume," which has been proven to spread aerosol droplets containing harmful pathogens.

The new center is very light on the land and provides a gateway into the restored wildlife habitat. Students go out in canoes with guides to see some 28 species of birds—four of which are on the National Audubon Society's watch list—that make their home on the Chesapeake Bay watershed. They also gain an understanding of "at-risk" species, such as the northern diamondback terrapin, a type of turtle that nests and forages along the bay's tidal marshes.

LEFT  **The center is powered by a 45-kilowatt array of PV panels installed on its southern-facing roof, and two 10-kilowatt wind turbines, which are set apart from the building in order to reduce disturbance and turbulence.**

OPPOSITE  **SmithGroup states that the curved zinc-coated roof is designed to mimic a fish's scales and recall the shimmering surface of the nearby water. On a functional level, the roof also channels rainwater into two cisterns for all the building's water uses.**

# Bullitt Center

Seattle, Washington, United States

OPPOSITE **The Bullitt Center** was designed to be the most sustainable commercial building in the world. The coplanar canopy roof, which looks like a graduation hat, holds 575 PV panels that generate 230 megawatt hours of energy annually.

RIGHT **To be a certified Living Building, none of the 360 hazardous materials found on the organization's "red list" can be used in the project. The Bullitt Center used 100 percent pure FSC-certified Douglas fir wood beams, columns, and flooring. All furniture, paints, coatings, carpets, adhesives, and fixtures are nontoxic.**

**The Bullitt Center in the Capitol Hill** neighborhood of Seattle, Washington, which opened in 2013, was designed to be the most sustainable commercial building in the world. Denis Hayes, CEO of the Bullitt Foundation, said the six-story, $32.5 million building was a "bold attempt to do everything right"—from net-zero energy and water use, to on-site composting of waste and the incorporation of healthy building materials. The center has a parking garage just for bicycles. And, amazingly, the primary structure was built to last 250 years, not the standard 40 years for commercial buildings. Given the amount of embodied carbon they contain, buildings that endure the longest are the most sustainable. And the Bullitt Center already stores 600 tons of carbon dioxide in its structural timber frame.

One of just a handful of commercial buildings to be certified through the stringent standards of the Living Building Challenge, the Bullitt Center achieves net-zero energy use through a rooftop array of PV panels, a ground source heating and cooling system, and inventive energy-efficiency approaches.

The first floor of the 52,000-square-foot (4,830-square-meter) center hosts the International Living Future Institute, which created the Living Building Challenge. On the second floor is the Center for Integrated Design, a program of the University of Washington Integrated Design Lab. The upper stories provide office space for engineering and technology firms.

According to the Miller Hull Partnership, the architects of the center, ambitious energy-efficiency measures were critical to ensuring the building could power itself. If the building used as much energy as a typical office building of the same size in Seattle, a gigantic 44,750-square-foot (4,150-square-meter) canopy would have been required for the PV panels. Instead, the architects were able to create a canopy 70 percent smaller with 575 SunPower panels that generate 230 megawatt hours of energy annually.

The Miller Hull Partnership modeled a range of configurations for the PV panels on the center's roofs and walls—from elevated and wall-mounted staggered arrays to ballasted roofs, from a vertical coplanar canopy to a continuous canopy. The team chose the coplanar canopy, which looks like a tilted graduation hat. Jim Hanford, a firm principal, said, "While the canopy doesn't deliver as much energy on a per panel basis, it produces the most amount of energy of all the options analyzed."

The Bullitt Center uses just 25 percent of the energy that a conventional building would use by incorporating a thermally efficient building envelope and curtain walls of triple-glazed windows. The tall and expansive windows naturally light Eighty-two percent of the interior spaces, thereby reducing the need for lighting energy. External window blinds are controlled by a building-management system that opens them to maximize daylight, when needed, and closes them to reduce solar heat gain and glare.

Heating and cooling are provided through radiant floor slabs integrated with ground-coupled heat pumps connected to 26 wells dug 400 feet (121 meters) deep. The center's operable windows allow for natural ventilation in all spaces.

According to Alex Ianchenko, a member of Miller Hull Partnership's architectural staff, the ventilation, heating, and cooling systems also make the building more resilient to SARS-CoV-2, the virus that causes COVID-19. The air-ventilation system uses 100 percent outside air and, therefore, does not recirculate air. Ianchenko explains that with the radiant floor-slab system, "heating and cooling also does not rely on air movement for delivery, so the building can condition the space without added mixing of air."

Furthermore, the building windows are programmed to automatically open at night during the summers, flushing out the air and precooling interior spaces before the workday begins. The automation system could be modified to open more often during the workday and during the year in order to bring in even more outside air for dilution.

The Bullitt Center is also designed to achieve net-zero water use. Gaps in the rooftop PV panels channel rainwater into downspouts that lead to a 56,000-gallon (212,000-liter) cistern in its basement. The center relies on filtered, treated rainwater for all purposes, including potable water.

Greywater from sinks and showers is directed to the constructed wetland. Waste from toilets is captured through 10 composters also found in the basement, which each generate 90 gallons (340 liters) of compost for nearby farms annually.

The Bullitt Center, which has a concrete foundation and floors, steel lateral braces, and a glued laminated Douglas fir timber frame, avoided some 362 common hazardous chemicals found in conventional building materials by using lead-free valves and fixtures, phthalate-free air membranes, neoprene-free EPDM couplings, PVC-free electrical wire, and VOC-free insulation adhesives along with other eco-friendly materials.

While most commercial buildings are designed with an economic life of 40 years, the Bullitt Foundation developed a structure that could last a quarter of a century. But convincing banks to finance a new commercial building with this lifespan proved to be a major challenge, so the foundation and Point32, the developer, put in more equity than originally anticipated, viewing it as an investment in the future. Without commercial buildings that push the boundaries, how can finance and development industries be persuaded to change?

RIGHT **External blinds on
the curtain walls of windows
are controlled by a building-
management system that either
opens them to maximize daylight
or closes them to reduce solar
heat gain and glare. 82 percent
of the interior spaces are
naturally daylit.**

BELOW **Instead of a conventional
parking garage for vehicles,
the Bullitt Center only includes
spaces for tenant bicycles,
reducing greenhouse gas
emissions from transportation.
The center took advantage of
new zero-parking allowances
in some of Seattle's denser
urban neighborhoods.**

# Pearl River Tower
## Guangzhou, China

The sleek, futuristic Pearl River Tower is one of the most sustainable supertall buildings in the world.

The 2,200-year-old port city of Guangzhou, China, approximately 80 miles (130 kilometers) from Hong Kong, is home to one of the most sustainable supertall towers in the world: the sleek, futuristic 1,013-foot-tall (309 meter) Pearl River Tower. Even in the skyscraper-laden Tianhe District, Skidmore, Owings & Merrill (SOM) and architects Adrian D. Smith and Gordon Gill created an aerodynamic, LEED Platinum–rated tower that turns heads. Thousands of PV panels and four embedded vertical-axis wind turbines demonstrate the good environmental intentions of the building. But it's actually the tower's internal energy-saving innovations that do the most to reduce energy use by 58 percent compared to the standard Chinese skyscraper.

The 2.58-million-square-foot (240,000-square-meter) commercial and office tower was built for the Guangzhou Pearl River Tower Properties Company, a subsidiary of a state-owned tobacco company, in 2011. SOM, Smith, and Gill worked with engineers at Rowan Williams Davies & Irwin to maximize the tower's ability to use both daylight and wind to generate energy. Through wind-tunnel modeling, they convinced the developer to orient the building to directly face southerly winds, which blow 80 percent of the year. The concave southern facade directs wind to two large openings on mechanical floors at the 25th and 50th stories, which house four wind turbines crafted by Windside. The wind is drawn through these openings, spinning the turbines as it exits through the north facade.

According to a case study in *High Performance Buildings*, wind speeds at those heights average 9 miles (14 kilometers) per hour. But given the wind is pulled into tighter corridors through negative pressure, the wind accelerates to up to 18 miles (29 kilometers) per hour, generating 15 times more power than stand-alone vertical turbines. The turbines, which have a combined generating capacity of 132 megawatt hours a year, were installed on the mechanical floors to reduce any noise, vibration, or safety issues and make maintenance easier.

There are approximately 16,000 square feet (1,480 square meters) of PV panels on the crown of the tower and an equal amount on shade structures on the east and west facades. Together, these panels generate an additional 200 megawatt hours of power annually. Much of the energy savings come from the interiors: radiant cooling systems and inventive double-skin windows with automated shading that controls daylight were installed on each of the 71 stories.

Two panes of glass that minimize ultraviolet and infrared light were sealed together, forming the exterior barrier. Those were then separated by a 9-inch (22.8-centimeter) air space from an interior layer of glass. This air gap draws humidity out of the interior spaces through a heat exchanger and also acts as a vent for hot air from within the building. Outside the windows on the northern and southern facades is an inventive automated shading system that tracks the angle and intensity of the sun in order to bring in light or shade interior spaces, maximizing the amount of daylight and the comfort of the office workers. The shading system is also designed to reduce the need for interior lighting and, therefore, energy use.

Instead of the fan coils, variable air volume boxes, filters, ductwork, and insulation found in typical interior heating and cooling systems, SOM and the rest of the design and engineering team flowed water through a radiant cooling system made of copper pipes in the ceiling. As a result, the building doesn't need much power or infrastructure to actively move, filter, heat, and cool recirculating interior air. A gap below each floor brings in fresh air that is then filtered and ventilated into each story. The radiant cooling system in the ceiling then cools the air, while vents let hot indoor air escape out of the building. This approach, which eliminates the need to install bulky traditional HVAC systems in each story, helped reduce the height of floors by nearly a foot (0.3 meters), saving five stories' worth of construction.

SOM and team sought to add microturbines (essentially a local power plant) within the base of the building, along with a geothermal heat-exchange system, which could have met 80 percent of the building's energy needs, but Guangzhou's regulations at the time prevented net-metering to sell energy back to the grid in commercial buildings. While SOM and the team weren't able to achieve a net-zero skyscraper, they came close through their imaginative design and engineering concepts.

OPPOSITE **Intensive modeling and design work resulted in an inventive, concave southern facade, where wind is directed to four openings—two on the 25th floor and two on the 50th floor. The wind passes through these openings, which house vertical-axis wind turbines that generate 132 megawatts of energy.**

TOP RIGHT **Automated shades manage the amount of daylight reaching the interior, optimizing comfort and helping to reduce use of interior lighting. Vents on each floor bring in fresh air that is then filtered and circulated. A radiant cooling system in each ceiling cools the space with water in copper coils, while hot air escapes through ceiling vents.**

BOTTOM LEFT **Sunshades and vents on the east and west facades of the tower are covered in PV panels.**

BOTTOM RIGHT **Four vertical-axis wind turbines by Windside— each 16 feet (5 meters) tall by 6.5 feet (2 meters) wide—meet approximately 5 percent of the tower's energy needs. The corridors through the tower were designed to compress and accelerate the flow of wind past the turbines.**

# Council House 2
## Melbourne, Australia

The western facade of the highly responsive CH2 government office is programmed to track the movement of the sun. In the winter, the recycled-wood shutters open to let in light; during peak afternoon sun in the summer, the shutters close.

**The city government of Melbourne,** Australia, has modeled the future with a unique office building: Council House 2 (CH2), which mimics the mutually supportive and responsive functions of an ecosystem. In a single building, CH2 encapsulates Melbourne's goal to marry sustainable buildings and nature to become a carbon-positive city by 2050.

Melbourne's city government, which is already carbon neutral in its operations, aims to decarbonize the entire city through 100 percent renewable energy, zero-emission buildings and precincts, zero-emission transportation, and waste reduction. Paired with these measures are ambitious efforts to sequester carbon and improve the health and well-being of residents by doubling the urban forest to 40 percent of the city by 2040 and covering buildings in green roofs, walls, and facades.

To achieve a zero-emission building sector, Melbourne has used its city-owned buildings as demonstration projects, showing the commercial sector how to meet the target of reducing greenhouse gas emissions by 25 percent. Other programs include more stringent energy-use requirements; retrofit financing available through a program that aims to retrofit 1,200 commercial buildings, which account for 70 percent of the city's commercial building stock; and incentives to incorporate natural systems, such as green roofs, to reduce building energy use.

The US$50 million CH2 was designed by Mick Pearce, an architect based in Zimbabwe, and Australian architecture firm DesignInc to function like an ecosystem, with "many parts that work together to heat, cool, power, and water the building, creating a harmonious environment." Like in an ecosystem, there is no waste and no single-function components.

In comparison with a conventional office building, CH2 has reduced greenhouse gas emissions by 87 percent, reduced energy and water use by 60 percent, and resulted in much higher levels of health and well-being for its 540 occupants. There are just 20 parking spaces for cars but 80 for cyclists and nine showers for their use.

The 134,500-square-foot (12,450-square-meter) 10-story building is porous and responsive to the surrounding environment. Its west facade is covered in recycled wood shutters programmed to track the sun; they close in the summer to block the strongest afternoon sun but open in the winter to warm the interior. On the northern facade, where the sun shines brightest in the southern hemisphere, vertical gardens provide shading, and pipes exhaust internal air. On the southern facade, vents draw in fresh air. And on the east facade, an abstracted perforated-steel wall provides exhaust from the bathrooms. The facades work together with the interior heating and cooling system, which leverages the thermodynamics of hot and cool airflow.

Whereas typical buildings use energy to heat and cool, circulate, and exhaust interior air, CH2 simply applies the laws of nature to draw in 100 percent fresh air, which is filtered and then distributed via vents on each floor. Gaps in ceilings then exhaust warm air, which is drawn out of six wind cowls on the roof. For air conditioning, air is drawn across curved chilled beams in the ceiling filled with cool water. At night, if the outside temperature is lower than the building's concrete structure, the building's window are programmed to open, which helps to remove the heat stored up by the thermal mass of the building during the course of the day. For warmth in the winter, air is prewarmed through a rooftop heat exchanger that captures heat from exhaust air.

There are also clear health benefits to CH2's approach to ventilation, heating, and cooling because the system does not recirculate air. Pearce explains, "With conventional HVAC systems, conditioned air can be recirculated six times before it is exhausted in order to save cooling energy. But recirculation can also cause 'building sickness syndrome,' as the ducts containing the circulating air collect unknown quantities of microorganisms [and viruses], like SARS-CoV-2, the virus that causes COVID-19, along with particulate matter, pollen, and other sources of unhealthy air. In the era of the coronavirus, I wonder whether office workers will start asking: 'Why aren't all office buildings designed like this? This must be safer than the conventional approach.'"

In the roof plant room, a cogeneration plant with a microturbine generates heat, steam, and electricity, improving energy efficiency because the energy doesn't need to travel far across the central grid to the building. The process generates waste heat and steam, which are captured and reused in the heating and cooling system. The rooftop has PV panels that generate another 3.5 kilowatts of power and solar water heaters that cover about 60 percent of the building's hot water

heating needs. When the building's elevators brake to stop, they also generate energy that is captured for building use.

CH2 provides the same amount of vegetation on its northern facade and green roof as would have been found on the site had it been undeveloped. Plant life is irrigated by rainwater captured on the roof, along with treated greywater from the building's sinks and showers, blackwater from its toilets, as well as 26 gallons (98 liters) of water mined from the sewage system each day.

An independent postoccupancy study found that after the first full year of operation, worker productivity improved nearly 11 percent. A key reason for the improved productivity is thought to be the high indoor air quality, which is the result of the fresh-air ventilation system and low-emission furniture and finishes. Exposed to natural light and filled with indoor plants, the building is perceived by workers to be a healthy work environment. More than 80 percent of occupants prefer CH2 to their previous office.

OPPOSITE **Fresh, filtered air is drawn into each office space through floor vents. The ceilings are curved to direct cooled air from panels of chilled beams to office workers and to help rising warm air exhaust through ceiling vents. CH2 includes low-emission furniture, carpeting, and finishes. The high quality of indoor air is seen as the primary cause of improved employee productivity.**

ABOVE **CH2's rooftop has a deck, gardens, PV panels, solar water heaters, and six yellow wind cowls, which use negative pressure to ventilate hot air from the building's interior. As the cowls spin, they also generate electricity.**

OPPOSITE **CH2 makes smart use of outside air to reduce energy use. Warm water is sprayed into "shower towers" that draw in air that is cooled through water evaporation. The cooler air is then channeled to the lower levels of the building as air conditioning, reducing the need to use energy to cool the spaces.**

RIGHT **In Australia, the fullest sun exposure comes from the north. On the north facade of CH2, breakout decks protect against a high-angle sun through a "light shelf," and climbing vines are used to protect against low-angle sun and glare.**

# Chapter Five

# POWER PLANTS

## Power Plants

—

### Geothermal, Solar, and Wind Power Facilities

Electricity generation accounts for 30 percent of global greenhouse gas emissions, making it the largest single source of emissions. For many decades, the primary source of power has been fossil fuels—coal, oil, and gas and, more recently, natural gas. Without a clear understanding of their dangerous impact on the climate and our health, we have used fossil fuels to power our homes, industry, and transportation systems. This is changing.

Today, some 33 percent of all electricity gener-ation worldwide is from renewable sources, with hydropower making up the majority of that 33 percent, followed by wind and then solar. Over the past decade, $3 trillion has been invested in clean power worldwide. In 2018, about two-thirds of new energy capacity installed was renewable.

According to a 2019 article by Niklas Höhne, Michel den Elzen, and others in the journal *Nature*, 76 countries or regions (the European Union being the largest) and 14 subnational regions or states (California being the largest) have set net-zero emission goals. Furthermore, 53 countries and 31 states and regions have "explicitly committed to an emissions-free electricity sector." In the US alone, 150 cities and 10 states and territories have mandated 100 percent renewable energy for electricity genera-tion, for some as early as 2032.

If we are going to keep warming below 1.5 degrees Celsius (2.7 degrees Fahrenheit), the best-case scenario outlined at the Paris Climate Accord, countries need to continue to ratchet up their mandates and enhance the policy and regulatory framework that incentivizes electricity from wind, water, and solar. The International Renewable Energy Agency states that investment in renewable energy needs to double over the next decade.

As Mark Z. Jacobson explains earlier in this book, there are multiple pathways to a 100 percent renewable electricity sector for every country in the world, and 10 countries have already achieved 100 percent: Costa Rica, Norway, Iceland, Albania, Paraguay, Uruguay, Tajikistan, Bhutan, Kenya, and Scotland. A number of European, African, Latin American, and Central Asian countries are also nearly there.

Over the next few decades, we will need to build thousands of new renewable energy power plants, including photovoltaic (PV) solar, geother-mal, wind, and hydropower facilities. In two-thirds of the world, solar and wind are already the cheapest energy option. To reduce coal and oil use, it's absolutely critical that electricity from renewable sources remain that way. Given the pressures of climate change, urban sprawl, and resource extraction on our remaining ecosystems, we must also limit the environmental and land-use impacts of the thousands of new facilities expected without delaying the transition to renewable energy.

In Power Plants, renewable energy projects around the world demonstrate smarter ways to design and build. Benefits can be achieved by decentralizing energy infrastructure and making it local, resilient, and equitable. Solar power plants can be built in or near urban areas to ensure the power generated is accessible and affordable to renters and low-income households.

Facilities can be planned and designed to reduce impacts on wildlife and, in some instances, even support ecological regeneration. These vital pieces of energy infrastructure can also be designed to reduce the visual impact on our cultural and natural landscapes. In fact, they can be designed to serve multiple functions and become real community assets.

The Suvilahti Solar Power Plant in Helsinki, Finland, is built atop a power station owned by Helen, Helsinki's power company. The project is marketed to energy consumers who can't afford to put PV panels on their roof or who don't have access because they rent. Through a website, consumers can choose their own solar panels and subscribe in just a few minutes. Their subscription is simply deducted from their energy bill. This solar power is made easily accessible to all.

Likewise, the Coyote Ridge Community Solar Farm in Fort Collins, Colorado, is designed to make the benefits of solar power more affordable. GRID Alternatives partnered with the Poudre Valley Rural Electric Association (PVREA) to build a community solar farm dedicated mostly to low-income residents, who see a 30 percent reduction in their annual energy bills. To construct the facility, GRID Alternatives brought in volunteers and job trainees to learn marketable skills in solar power installation.

The Block Island Wind Farm off the coast of Rhode Island is a model of how to site an offshore wind farm to minimize bird fatalities and other environmental impacts. The facility demonstrates the value of a comprehensive ecological-planning approach with private and public stakeholders, which should be followed for the 30 additional offshore wind projects now planned along the Eastern Seaboard.

Providing a persuasive contribution, Rob Davis, director of the Center for Pollinators in Energy at Fresh Energy, a nonprofit based in Saint Paul, Minnesota, makes the case for transforming sites for solar power facilities into sanctuaries for pollinators. Insect pollinators—bees in particular—are dying off at an unsustainable rate around the world. Numerous states in the US have now created standards that enable solar power facilities to support increasingly fragile bumblebee, honeybee, and monarch butterfly populations, as well as those of other native bees.

Solar power sites can support multiple goals, including ecological regeneration. In another fascinating contribution, Björk Guðmundsdóttir, a landscape architect with Landsvirkjun, Iceland's national power company, walks through her company's renewable-energy-design policy, which is one of the most progressive in the world. After a public backlash over the environmental impact of a hydropower project, Landsvirkjun redesigned its approach to renewable energy infrastructure projects. Utility-scale hydropower and geothermal projects must now be designed in harmony with the landscape and provide community benefits. Geothermal and hydropower plants in planning stages throughout Iceland show how to marry infrastructure with landscape design, ecological restoration, and placemaking. One planned power plant even includes a hotel and greenhouse.

# Block Island Wind Farm
Block Island, Rhode Island, United States

**The United Kingdom, Germany,** and China are the current leaders in offshore wind power, with a combined capacity of nearly 19 gigawatts in 2018. But the US plans to catch up. Ambitious plans are underway to build up to 30 offshore wind farms along the East Coast from Maryland to North Carolina, which together could generate 25 gigawatts of energy.

On the Eastern Seaboard, the project that led the way is the five-turbine, 30-megawatt Block Island Wind Farm off the coast of Rhode Island, which began transmitting power in 2016. The economic purpose of the wind farm is to provide cheaper renewable electricity to Block Island, 13 miles from the coast of Rhode Island, which had long been dependent on dirty and expensive diesel fuel. Planned and built by Deepwater Wind (now operated by Ørsted US Offshore Wind), the wind farm is a model for siting turbines for minimal impact on birds and shows the value of a comprehensive ecological-planning approach between public and private stakeholders.

### The Best Way to Reduce Bird Collisions with Wind Turbines: Smart Siting

A 2013 study by Scott Loss, Tom Will, and Peter P. Marra in the journal *Biological Conservation* found that onshore wind farms kill somewhere between 140,000 and 328,000 birds annually. With the potential expansion of offshore wind facilities along the East Coast, migratory birds that use the Atlantic Flyway could face similar or even greater collision rates if projects aren't well sited. In addition, offshore wind facilities can displace some species of seabirds from prime foraging and nesting areas.

A landmark study published in *Science* in 2019 found there are an estimated 3 billion fewer birds in the US than there were 50 years ago, marking a decline in their population of nearly 30 percent. Widespread use of pesticides and habitat loss were identified as the greatest causes of these declines. Additionally, the US Fish and Wildlife Service found that the loss, degradation, or fragmentation of millions of acres of bird habitat each year is caused by development, agriculture, and forestry practices. Climate change is also significantly accelerating the degradation and destruction of bird habitats. For example, sea-level rise means the loss of vital coastal habitat and wetland ecosystems, which will impact a wide range of bird species. Other significant human-made causes of bird fatalities include ubiquitous glass buildings, vehicles on roads, utility lines, and communication towers.

Given the incredible challenges birds already face, there is no reason why the transition to renewable energy should add to the problem. According to conservation groups, such as the American Bird Conservancy and the National Audubon Society, the most effective way to reduce bird deaths by wind farms is to site these facilities outside areas important for birds, such as migratory corridors and stopover points and feeding and nesting areas. Wind availability and land-development costs alone can't be the sole determinants of where to build wind farms.

### A Model for Offshore Wind Farm Planning and Siting

Planning for the Block Island Wind Farm was led by the Rhode Island Coastal Resources Management Council (CRMC), which assembled experts from academic institutions, including the University of Rhode Island, to undertake a two-year planning effort to map opportunities and constraints in an area covering approximately 1,500 square miles (3,800 square kilometers) off the coast of Rhode Island. The teams analyzed where wind was strongest; where it was feasible to lay transmission cables and build foundations for the turbines; the extent and type of whale, fish, and bird life in the study

**The five-turbine Block Island Wind Farm generates and transmits 20 megawatts of renewable energy to Block Island, a community 13 miles off the coast of Rhode Island.**

ABOVE **After a comprehensive two-year ecological-planning effort, involving public and private stakeholders, the Block Island Wind Farm was carefully sited some 3.8 miles (6.1 kilometers) southeast from Block Island in Rhode Island state waters.**

OPPOSITE **In 2016, five awe-inspiring Alstom Wind (now GE Wind) Haliade 150-6 MW turbines were installed by Deepwater Wind. Each turbine stands 600 feet (180 meters) and has a 492-foot (150-meter) rotor diameter that creates a 190,000-square-foot (17,680-square-meter) rotor-swept area.**

area; current sport, whale watching, and dive sites; scenic viewsheds that needed to be preserved; and commercial fishing areas, among other factors. The result of their work was the Ocean Special Area Management Plan (Ocean SAMP), a sort of marine zoning plan for offshore wind that was applauded by President Barack Obama's Ocean Policy Task Force.

As part of the Ocean SAMP, a team of researchers at the University of Rhode Island's Department of Natural Resources Science undertook surveys on land, by boat, and by air in order to create a spatial map of bird life in the study area, including data such as mean numbers of birds, distribution areas, flight altitudes of species, and the relationships between bathymetry and bird life. Bird flight altitudes were studied to determine which species fly at the same altitude as wind-turbine rotor-swept areas, or the area carved out by the rotor's range, and would therefore be at greatest risk of collision. The study also attempted to understand where wind farm installation and operation would cause the least disturbance to habitat.

Over 13 months and nearly eight hundred shore-based sea watches, the research team detected 141 bird species; from 54 ship-based surveys, some 56 species; and from 10 aerial surveys, 17 species or guilds of birds. A cornucopia of avian life was detected: loons, grebes, shearwaters, storm petrels, gannets, cormorants, sea ducks, jaegers, gulls, kittiwakes, terns, alcids, and passerines. Of special interest was the endangered roseate tern, which was seen 125 times in the northwest corridor of the study area.

The Ocean SAMP overlays data about migratory routes, feeding, and breeding areas of multiple key species of birds, identifying high- and low-risk zones. According to Professor Peter Paton at the University of Rhode Island, an ornithologist who led the avian component of the plan, the Ocean SAMP "brought together all the key players and was an excellent example of how to plan the location of a wind farm that minimizes impacts on birds. The wind farm was placed at a site that had a relatively low probability of impacting bird populations."

In 2016, five Alstom Wind (now GE Wind) Haliade 150-6 MW turbines were installed by Deepwater Wind some 3.8 miles (6.1 kilometers) southeast from Block Island in Rhode Island state waters. Each turbine stands 600 feet tall (180 meters) and has a 492-foot (150-meter) rotor diameter that creates a 190,000-square-foot (17,680-square-meter) rotor-swept area.

According to Joel Merriman, director of the Bird-Smart Wind Energy Campaign at the American Bird Conservancy, the study of bird life organized by the CRMC was important because bird-collision risk is complex and requires deeper analysis. "Some species fly below the rotor-swept area during breeding season but may fly at different heights during migration," Merriman notes. "Other birds, such as some species of shearwaters or petrels, may fly at different heights due to weather conditions. Flocks of songbirds make overnight flights over the water, potentially placing them in harm's way with wind facilities. Others are known to avoid offshore facilities all together, essentially resulting in habitat loss." As a result, "it is crucial for facilities to be sited appropriately, based on robust data examining the year-round presence and behavior patterns of birds in the area. Unfortunately, there's no one-size-fits-all model."

### Scaling up Rhode Island's Approach to the Entire East Coast

With more offshore wind farms coming to the East Coast, it's important that ecological planning continues in federal and state waters. Planning can result in intentional placement of turbines with appropriate heights and rotor diameters.

A study commissioned by the US Department of Interior's Bureau of Ocean Energy Management (BOEM), released in 2019, examined how endangered terns and threatened piping plovers could be impacted by wind farms in the wind-energy areas designated by the BOEM that have been leased to offshore wind facility developers.

As part of data collection for the study, which occurred from 2014 to 2017, hundreds of roseate terns, common terns, and piping plovers were fitted with very high frequency (VHF) transmitters, and their flight paths and altitudes were analyzed. The report found that an estimated 20 percent of piping plover flights occurred within the rotor-swept zone, while just 4 percent of common tern flights and 6 percent of roseate tern flights did. The data shows the need for placing the new wind farms outside their migratory routes and feeding areas. The authors also call for installing VHF trackers on offshore wind turbines, which would allow the trackers to pick up signals from transmitters on the birds and help solve the problem of bird fatalities.

OPPOSITE TOP **The northeast US population of roseate terns is endangered. In Europe, the largest populations of these fierce seabirds are found in Ireland, but they also nest in Iceland and the United Kingdom. In the UK, they are designated for protection under the Biodiversity Action Plan because climate change is a threat to their food sources.**

OPPOSITE BOTTOM LEFT **As part of the ecological-planning process for Block Island Wind Farm, ornithologists at the University of Rhode Island identified and analyzed the coastal nesting areas of the roseate tern. The turbines were purposefully sited far away from these areas to minimize impacts on their remaining populations.**

OPPOSITE BOTTOM RIGHT **This charming piping plover has been banded, which helps government agencies, scientists, and conservation organizations track and protect them. Other plovers have been tagged with nanotags and small, thin antennae to track their flight paths and altitudes. An understanding of how these threatened birds behave will help better site offshore wind farms to minimize collisions.**

# Coyote Ridge Community Solar Farm

Fort Collins, Colorado, United States

**Vara Vissa was one of three hundred** volunteers and job trainees who helped build the Poudre Valley Rural Electric Association (PVREA) Coyote Ridge Community Solar Farm, a 1.95-megawatt energy system designed to benefit low-income residents in Fort Collins, Colorado. The solar array was built over just two months in 2017 on 9 acres (3.6 hectares) next to the Larimer County Landfill. Developing the power plant on an already-disturbed site reduced any further environmental impact on the surrounding grass ecosystem.

GRID Alternatives Colorado, an affiliate of nonprofit GRID Alternatives, received a $1.2 million grant from the Colorado Energy Office (CEO) to build a set of community solar farms at different sizes and with multiple financing approaches to demonstrate how to reduce costs for "utilities' highest-need customers." These are customers who earn 80 percent or less of the median area income and typically spend 4 percent or more of their income on utility bills. The community solar farms aim to complement the CEO's statewide weatherization program.

For this community solar installation, GRID Alternatives Colorado partnered with PVREA, a rural energy cooperative, in order to make clean energy more accessible and affordable to all. Through an innovative approach, 700 kilowatts of capacity were dedicated to low-income customers, 500 kilowatts were dedicated to nonprofits, and the remaining 750 kilowatts were made available to all other customers. All participants contribute financially through an on-bill financing model.

The largest facility GRID Alternatives has developed to date, Coyote Ridge Community Solar Farm supports about 140 low-income customers at a time, who participate in five-year terms and pay no upfront fees. Their annual utility bills are offset by 30 percent, representing $660,000 in estimated savings over the project's 20-year lifespan.

According to America's Electrical Cooperatives, by mid-2018, an estimated 85 percent of Coyote Ridge's solar panels reserved for low-income residents had been subscribed, in comparison to 49 percent of panels for traditional subscribers and 38 percent of panels for nonprofits, such as schools and firehouses.

The CEO and the PVREA partnered with GRID Alternatives in part because GRID Alternatives also adopts an equitable approach to building community solar facilities. They bring in large numbers of volunteers, who help implement the solar arrays in a low-cost manner, thereby passing savings on to energy customers.

Assisting the engineers and technicians, the volunteers and job trainees gained marketable new skills as part of solar-installation job training. At Coyote Ridge, volunteers helped set up some six thousand tilting panels that follow the sun.

Students at the Colorado School of Mines were also able to participate. Mechanical engineering student Evan Wong told GRID Alternatives: "In the classroom we learn about quantum mechanics and circuitry and spend hours and hours studying it. Seeing the tracking mechanism and all the tiny parts gave a great real world experience."

GRID Alternatives states that since 2004, they have reduced energy costs through solar access for more than 15,000 households, saving an estimated $380 million; assisted 111 community facilities, such as affordable multifamily housing complexes, in transitioning to clean energy; and engaged more than 43,000 people in solar education and training.

Their work has produced 1.87 billion kilowatt hours of clean energy, which will prevent 985,000 tons of greenhouse gas emissions over a 25-year period, equal to taking 188,000 cars off the road. The Coyote Ridge Community Solar Farm also won the Smart Electric Power Alliance's 2018 Electric Cooperative Utility of the Year award.

OPPOSITE **Just to the south of the Larimer County Landfill, the Poudre Valley Rural Electric Association (PVREA) Coyote** **Ridge Community Solar Farm features 6,000 panels that tilt to follow the sun.**

BELOW **Engineers and technicians guide volunteers in laying out the solar farm's structure, which supports 6,000 panels.**

RIGHT **Vara Vissa, who is a board member for the Air Quality Advisory Board of Fort Collins and lives less than a mile away from Coyote Ridge Community Solar Farm, volunteered for three days on-site. She commented,** "This is a lovely, positive image for me, something that my family and community can benefit from. To see it being installed and being a part of it makes it all come together for me."

COYOTE RIDGE COMMUNITY SOLAR FARM

# Suvilahti Solar Power Plant

Helsinki, Finland

In 2017, the city of Helsinki, the capital of Finland, sped up its goal to become carbon neutral by 15 years: instead of achieving carbon neutrality by 2050, the city of 650,000 would meet the target by 2035. A year later, a cross-departmental government group released a detailed plan with 143 actions to reduce greenhouse gas emissions by 80 percent and offset the other 20 percent.

The bulk of Helsinki's emissions come from heating buildings during the long, cold winters. The plan found that a 20 percent cut in emissions from heating could be achieved through retrofitting older buildings to be more energy efficient and designing all new buildings to be net-zero through the use of solar and geothermal energy sources. Other heating-related greenhouse gas emissions have to be tackled at the source of energy production. Helen, the city-owned energy company, which provides energy, heating, and cooling to 90 percent of the city's buildings, has been deriving half of its energy from coal and another third from natural gas.

As part of the city's plan, Helen drew up a bold strategy to transition its citywide energy sources to 70 percent renewable by 2035. Helen will shut down its coal-powered Hanasaari power plant, develop a heat-pump power plant that reuses waste heat from the city's wastewater-treatment system, and expand locally produced solar power and energy-storage systems.

There are a number of benefits to creating solar power plants in urban environments. Building solar farms on brownfields and the rooftops of industrial, commercial, and residential buildings eliminates the need to create sprawling fields of concentrated solar thermal or PV-panel power plants that negatively impact wildlife. Urban solar energy is generated close to where it will be used, reducing transmission costs. Many homeowners and commercial property owners don't have structures that can bear the weight of solar panels or the wherewithal to install them. Neighborhood-scale power plants can be more inclusive. And in an era of rising seas and powerful storms, local renewable-power-generation and energy-storage systems increase community resilience to natural disasters.

In 2018, Helen opened the Suvilahti solar power plant on the roof of one of its substations in Helsinki. Its 1,194 PV panels, with an output of 275 kilowatts, now power more than one hundred one-bedroom apartments.

Helen also attached panels to the front of the substation, creating a distinctive solar wall with an additional 84 panels that generate an output of 24 kilowatts.

Helen made the PV panels directly accessible to its customers, who can subscribe to specific panels at Suvilahti via an easy-to-use website at a monthly cost of €4.40 (US$5) per panel. Helen sells the approach this way: "With a designated panel, you can start producing solar energy without purchasing a solar panel. Renting a panel is a good solar energy solution for people living in a block of flats or terraced house or for a small-business owner."

Helen states that a typical customer in a one-bedroom apartment that subscribes to five panels at a cost of €22 (US$25), or €264 (US$296) annually, can meet their own energy needs. The customers' subscription fees are deducted from their energy bills. A review of the power plant's website found that as of December 2019, there were just 15 panels available out of the 1,194. Given the success of the project, Helen built a larger plant in the Kivikko district with three thousand panels that can generate an output of 850 kilowatts.

OPPOSITE The Suvilahti solar power plant is found on the roof of a substation owned by Helen, the city-owned electric utility. The 1,192 panels have an output of 275 kilowatts, providing power for 100 nearby homes. Customers who may not be able to or cannot afford to install solar panels on their own roof can subscribe to designated panels for a monthly fee.

OPPOSITE **Helen also installed 84 panels with an output of 24 kilowatts on the front of the substation, creating a solar wall that sends a clear public signal that all available urban spaces can be used to generate renewable power.**

RIGHT **Given that the energy generated by the rooftop PV panels is generated during the day, thousands of batteries within the substation store power for use at night. The bulk of energy is also generated during Finland's spring and summer, so energy must be stored for use in the winter.**

BOTTOM **Within the substation, rows of inverters transform the direct current output from the PV panels into alternating current that can be used by homeowners and property owners. Inverters also monitor the performance of the panels, ensuring they function at maximum levels.**

**Voices from the Field**

# Landsvirkjun's Renewable Energy Design Policy

Iceland

—

by Björk Guðmundsdóttir

OPPOSITE **Iceland covers 39,700 square miles (103,000 square kilometers). Its landscape is characterized by large, bare open areas. Only a fourth of the island is vegetated. Lowland areas have sparse vegetation, and the highlands (656 feet to 1,968 feet [200 to 600 meters] above sea level) are mostly nonvegetated, except for moss that forms in the lava deserts.**

RIGHT **The summers in Iceland are short and bright, and the winters are long and dark. In the winter, the aurora borealis (northern lights) appears when conditions are right.**

Iceland, a volcanic island located in the North Atlantic Ocean just south of the Arctic Circle, is among the few countries in the world that generates nearly all of its electricity from renewable sources, such as hydropower, geothermal energy, and, recently, a bit of wind power.

Electrification in Iceland began one hundred years ago. The first power plant serving the public was a 9-kilowatt hydroelectric power station built in Hafnarfjördur in 1904. Landsvirkjun, the national power company, was founded in 1965 and now has 18 power stations across the country that provide electricity for the country's 350,000 residents and the millions of tourists who visit each year. Landsvirkjun produces 72 percent of the country's electricity, approximately 18 terawatt hours.

One of the central goals of Landsvirkjun, the national power company, is to operate in harmony with nature and the landscape. Power projects in Iceland are mostly located in the highlands, where there is scarce vegetation, desert fields made of lava, and Mars-like black sand, glaciers, lagoons, and rivers. Within these expansive landscapes, structures can be highly visible.

The same elements that make the Icelandic landscape so fascinating also create great challenges in designing renewable energy power plants. The dilemma for a landscape architect is whether to hide or reveal the power infrastructure in nature.

### Achieving a New Strategic Design Policy

The legal framework in Iceland is similar to frameworks in Western Europe and the US. Iceland also has a national planning strategy and master plan for natural protection and energy use. By law, utilities must carry out environmental-impact assessments before initiating large-scale developments. There are also regional plans, municipal master plans, local plans, and development permits.

Landsvirkjun was heavily criticized for its 690-megawatt hydropower plant in Fljótsdalshérað (Kárahnjúkavirkjun) in eastern Iceland. Amid the public backlash, the company realized it was necessary to bring a stronger sustainability mindset to the planning and design of power plants.

Among several actions, in 2012 the company decided to establish a role for a landscape architect within its environmental department. Initial questions that arose included: What role can a landscape architect play in a power company? How should design recommendations be made, and how should collaboration with engineers happen? Should the goal be to hide all power-generation structures in the open, vulnerable landscape, or should they be visible, revealing their purpose?

The first thing to decide was the vision. The company determined that every power plant needed to reflect a sense of place and feel like it belongs to the landscape. The new design policy had to be strategic and not too specific. But the planning and design of each power project would need to be specific to each site. The policy had to anticipate projects' entire life cycles. The policy had to make use of the planning and design professions but also adhere to company policies and enable collaboration with communities demanding solutions that fit their needs. The policy had to provoke innovation.

Internal acceptance of the new policy required countless consultations and reviews. In 2016, the strategic policy for landscape architecture and architectural design was approved. The purpose of the policy is to achieve a balance between architecture and landscape architecture and the natural landscape. There are eight guidelines to achieve that balance:

1. The site location, landscape design, and layout of structures will take into account nature, sense of place, and characteristics of the landscape at each location.

2. Professional design will be used to create design principles. Design will be interwoven with necessary elements: art, technology, usability, creativity, ingenuity, and cultural heritage. Relevant professional groups will work together on a common path, informing choices of structures and designs.

3. In preliminary phases of power projects, design concepts will be produced to create harmony over the lifetime of the project. This approach will be reviewed regularly and updated through the project's preparation process, if deemed necessary.

4. Historical structures, cultural landscapes, and the environment will be evaluated, so that protection, maintenance, or possible restoration will be ensured in parallel with development.

5. Landscape assessment will be carried out as one of the baselines for preparing proposals for energy projects.

6. Sustainable design methods will support planning, design, and construction.

7. Planning will endorse multipurpose land use and sustainable opportunities.

8. Emphasis is placed on instituting design competition, where appropriate.

Landsvirkjun has defined five stages for the development and construction of new power plants: feasibility study, preliminary study, design, construction, and operations. The new strategic design policy guides all stages.

As part of its corporate social responsibility goals, Landsvirkjun also engages with the public and key stakeholders throughout every project. The majority of community engagement occurs in the project planning and design stages as part of the legal environmental-impact-assessment process. Based on the recommendations from national authorities and input from communities, plans are reviewed and revisions or mitigations made.

**Design Policy in Action**

The design policy has been put in action to shape two power plants now in development: a future geothermal plant and the Hvammsvirkjun hydropower plant. The future geothermal power plant is the first project being developed from the preliminary planning phase with the new guidelines. These early concepts show how integrated, adaptive, and collaborative solutions created by landscape architects and architects can enhance a geothermal power station located in

**LEFT** The Icelandic landscape is shaped by the forces of nature, from glaciers to active volcanoes. Volcanoes have created the vast lava fields and black-sand beaches. Underground lava flows generate heat and steam, which create geothermal energy.

**BELOW** Snow-capped mountains and glaciers feed into glacial lagoons, such as Jökulsárlón. Iceland has a freshwater landscape made up of rivers, streams, ponds, hot springs, and waterfalls. Iceland generates approximately 75 percent of its electricity from hydropower.

an environmentally sensitive area. The designs show how to marry infrastructure with placemaking. Designs can achieve wider public acceptance if they provide multiple services and economic opportunities. Also, because most of the proposed power plants are located aboveground and are highly visible, it is necessary to carefully design the landscapes and incorporate high-quality architecture that reinforces buildings' horizontal forms, visually anchoring them to the landscape.

To achieve these objectives and gain new ideas, the company has involved several landscape architecture and architecture firms in power plant design. For the future geothermal plant, the designers Arkís and A2F architects both came up with a proposal, each with great potential but very different in nature. The architects were asked to embrace Landsvirkjun's new strategic-design policy; create harmony between the layout, scale, and facade of buildings and the Icelandic landscape; create an architectural style of building with the ambience of a "mountain hut"; integrate multiple uses for tourists and recreational activities; and be sustainable and creative.

Even though the tender phase design for a hydropower project at Hvammsvirkjun had already been finalized, the decision was made to revise the landscape and architectural design to meet the new guidelines and achieve a greater balance with the environment. Revisions were done by VA Architects and the landscape architecture firm Landark, resulting in a greater connection to the surrounding landscape, the restoration of the disrupted land around the structures, enhanced accessibility for both pedestrians and horseback riders, and improvements in the form and materials in the power plant structures. Landscape architecture firm Land Use Consultants further enhanced the landscape design.

### Planning and Designing *with* the Landscape

A clear understanding of the nature of a landscape must be gained at the earliest stage of a project. Landscape-led design is an approach rooted in the local sense of place, a design that reflects a place's underlying character rather than imposing upon it. A comprehensive landscape character assessment is crucial to this approach. Assessments should take into account both natural and human factors and consider physical, cultural, and aesthetic aspects.

Landscape assessments contribute to all stages of the project, from early feasibility work through detail design to assessment and implementation. At each stage, it is important to revisit the landscape baseline to address any changes or new insights into the character of the place.

The design and assessment processes are connected in an iterative cycle of improvement. Design solutions should be tested against the landscape baseline and refined until an optimized scheme is developed that successfully balances the needs of the community with the demands of the landscape. This iterative approach can be applied to all aspects of power project design: from siting and deciding on its form and positioning to the use of materials and colors.

The approach does not mean that bold design statements must be avoided, only that they must arise from the project context, rather than being imposed from the outside. By creating designs sympathetic to the landscape, projects can provide multiple benefits in terms of biodiversity, energy production, recreation, tourism, and heritage preservation, resulting in genuinely sustainable solutions.

*Björk Guðmundsdóttir is a chartered landscape architect in the environment department at Landsvirkjun, Iceland's national power company. She is a member of the Icelandic Landscape Architects Association (FÍLA) and a delegate for FÍLA with the International Federation of Landscape Architects in Europe. Guðmundsdóttir has more than 20 years of experience in environmental mitigation, landscape and visual assessment, and planning. Her focus is on collaborating with stakeholders and the public to formulate planning and design proposals that achieve sustainability by balancing environmental, social, and economic needs.*

RIGHT **A conceptual design for a multiuse facility in the highlands of Iceland. A geothermal power plant also includes housing for plant staff, a hotel, and spa.**

BOTTOM LEFT **The multiuse facility could also include greenhouses for growing fruit and vegetables for both the geothermal power plant workers and the hotel guests.**

BOTTOM RIGHT **The horizontal form of the geothermal power plant mimics the surrounding mountains, helping the facility blend into the landscape.**

ABOVE **A design for a geothermal power plant that blends into the landscape.**

LEFT **The same view covered in snow during Iceland's winter.**

OPPOSITE **Updated designs for a hydropower plant facility that blends into the surrounding landscape through the use of horizontal forms and simple, natural materials.**

# Solar Sanctuaries for Pollinators
## United States (various states)
—

by Rob Davis

In researching how to make solar energy more compatible with agriculture and ecosystems, policy advocates in Minnesota were inspired by the Westmill Solar Park in Watchfield, England, which has a 5-megawatt capacity.

Encouraged by research from Lancaster University, the UK Solar Trade Association and developers, like Eden Renewables, encourage the use of pollinator-friendly vegetation.

**John Jacob of Old Sol Apiaries in** Oregon's Rogue Valley arranges his newest bee yard among millions of emerging flowers and native grasses. Looking around appreciatively, he knows the site will provide healthy food for his bees and never be sprayed with insecticides—his yard is adjacent to millions of dollars' worth of PV solar panels on racks a few feet off the ground.

While Jacob works, the ground-mounted solar panels silently convert light from Earth's "old Sol" directly into electricity for nearby schools, businesses, and residents, as well as generating revenue that pays ecologists to manage the acres of flowering yarrow, blue-eyed Mary, Oregon sunshine, rose checkermallow, and other ground cover throughout the site.

Halfway across the country in Saint Joseph, Minnesota, Dustin Vanasse of Bare Honey places groups of honeybee hives adjacent to more than a dozen flowering, pollinator-friendly solar farms. Over three years, Vanasse and entomology graduate students will monitor honey production and the health of the hives, conducting research similar to studies from other agricultural lands that have quantified the benefits of meadow habitat to crops, soils, and ecosystems.

Through close collaboration with companies, including Engie, Enel Green Power, and US Solar Corporation, and energy policy advocates, like Fresh Energy, beekeepers across the country are accelerating the use of ecological PV solar power plant designs that establish acres of flowering meadows under and around the panels. The pollinator-friendly designs aren't just enjoyed by bees—Bare Honey and Old Sol, as well as Vermont's Bee the Change, are delighting customers, partners, and leading researchers with honey that is "solar grown." They are also collaborating with breweries, cideries, and restaurants to use the honey as a hero ingredient.

Recipient of the MacArthur Foundation's "Genius" award, Dr. Marla Spivak, of the University of Minnesota Bee Lab, sees a promising opportunity. "It would be great to have pollinator habitat under and around solar panels and arrays."

## Solar Bloom

Driven by rapidly declining costs and corporate and municipal 100 percent clean-energy commitments, demand for large-scale solar energy development is surging. The National Renewable Energy Laboratory (NREL) forecasts that farmers and other landowners will lease 2 to 3 million acres (809,000 to 1,214,000 hectares) of land for ground-mounted solar arrays by 2030, a tenfold increase from 2020.

This rapid bloom in leasing land to produce solar energy isn't just a lifeline for farmers looking to stabilize on-farm

In St. Joseph, Minnesota, Bare Honey manages hives of honeybees located adjacent to pollinator-friendly solar farms. Solar companies and electric utilities, like Connexus Energy and IPS Solar, value that Bare Honey has a fully licensed and insured food-safe handling and packaging process. Bare Honey's customers for Solar Grown honey include breweries, like 56 Brewing and Voodoo Brewing, and specialty food retailers, like Clif Family Winery.

income—it's also a once-in-a-generation opportunity to create habitat at a large scale to help species critical to agriculture and ecosystem health. Climate change and loss of habitat pose significant threats to honeybees and bumblebees, monarch butterflies, and a wide variety of pollinators. A 2016 global analysis found that 40 percent of pollinator species may be at risk of extinction in the coming years.

Pollinator-friendly solar development is the practice of making meaningful, incremental changes to seed-mix design and vegetation-management practices in order to benefit managed and native pollinating insects and other wildlife. With prominent feature stories in *Fast Company*, *Scientific American*, and *Solar Power World* and webinars by the National Conservation Training Center, International Society of Sustainability

Professionals, and the NREL, PV facility designs optimized for pollinator-friendly ground cover is fast becoming a best practice.

For utilities and other solar electricity buyers, the land under and around these sites presents an opportunity to realize the ancillary benefits to ecological resilience and corporate social responsibility while also reducing the total cost of ownership and the cost of energy produced.

## From Solarcentric to Solar Sanctuaries for Pollinators

Because the US solar industry first took off in the desert of the Southwest in the United States, standard practices for the land on solar sites have included bare ground, gravel, and shallow-rooted lawn grass. These "solarcentric" designs prioritize the solar configuration and give comparatively little consideration

to land stewardship and other environmental and agricultural factors.

At the same time solar was taking off in the Southwest, solar was also growing rapidly in England and Germany, though with radically different engineering and design principles. With equal priority given to agricultural functions and enhancing biodiversity, solar sites with flowering low-growing meadows under and around the panels became a common practice.

As solar became cost competitive outside of the Southwest, these practices were noticed—particularly in the Midwest. In 2015, a group of energy, agriculture, and conservation policy leaders came together in Minnesota to establish the nation's first statewide standard for the vegetation that grows under and around large ground-mounted solar sites. The following

Minnesota Native Landscapes' flocks of sheep have put in more than one million "sheep hours" grazing on solar farms, including Enel Green Power's 150 megawatt Aurora solar facility pictured here. As recommended by the American Solar Grazing Association, the shepherd uses rotational grazing, a practice praised for its effectiveness in supporting biodiversity and sequestering carbon.

In Downsville, Wisconsin, ENGIE, one of the world's largest independent power producers, uses pollinator-friendly ground cover as a standard practice on its solar farms developed on arable land.

year, the coalition unanimously passed the Pollinator-Friendly Solar Act into law. In the years since, several other states (New York, Maryland, South Carolina, Vermont, Illinois, Missouri, Ohio, Michigan, Virginia, North Carolina, Indiana) have adopted similar standards to help ensure productive use of the land under and around solar facilities.

Implementation is straightforward—ensure the lower edge of the solar panels is 3.2 feet (1 meter) above the ground, have an ecologist design a seed mix suitable for the local soil and climate conditions, then hire a landscape manager with meadow and native plant experience.

Simple dos and don'ts of pollinator-friendly solar:

- Do bury all the cabling; don't string it aboveground, blocking the rows.
- Do use a deer- or livestock-style fence; don't use a prison-style chain-link fence.
- Do mount the PV panels at least 3.2 feet (one meter) above the ground; don't put panels so low that frequent mowing is required, increasing mower and PV-panel collision risk.
- Do use a cover crop to stabilize soil and meet stormwater permit requirements while the pollinator seed mix gets established.

## Productive Land Use

For the agricultural and conservation stakeholders, it has been important to ensure the standards would result in more than a green veneer and provide meaningful benefits to pollinators within the operating constraints of the solar-energy-generation facility. "We're not talking about just a narrow row of native vegetation by the front gate that makes it look like a project is pollinator-friendly," said Laura Caspari, a director with ENGIE, a company that has adopted pollinator-friendly development principles across its portfolio. "That's why the standards are so important, because they provide a benchmark."

New development, even of a solar power facility, on land that has grown corn, beans, cotton, or hay for a generation can result in people mistakenly thinking that using some farmland for solar threatens the food supply. But beekeepers and other conservation advocates have consistently highlighted the grave risk to food systems from lack of available healthy forage for pollinators.

Producing a single market-ready blueberry requires a pollinator to visit a flower two to four times, which sounds easy enough. But there are

Signage and fencing are also important design considerations. Clif Bar & Company has a pollinator-friendly solar farm adjacent to its bakery in Twin Falls, Idaho, that includes interpretive signage by designer Arlene Birt and a walking path. Deer- and livestock-style fencing are cost competitive with chain-link fencing and are significantly more aesthetically appealing.

The National Renewable Energy Laboratory's Jordan Macknick (right) is the principal investigator of the InSPIRE study, a 20-site national study funded by the US Department of Energy into low-impact solar designs, including pollinator-friendly solar. Enel Green Power's Aurora solar project in Minnesota, pictured, is part of the study.

1 to 5 million flowers per acre of blueberries, and all 64,000 acres (25,900 hectares) grown in the US are flowering around the same time. The story is similar for other crops. Each raspberry flower requires five to six pollinator visits to produce a marketable fruit. Each strawberry, 20 to 60 visits. These crops, and others, produce hundreds of billions of individual flowers, requiring trillions and trillions of visits by managed and native pollinators each year. In order to sustain these pollinators throughout the year, they need acres of healthy habitat for the times when the crops aren't blooming.

In addition to helping pollinator populations, Clare Lindahl, CEO of the Soil and Water Conservation Society, sees the significant opportunity to benefit farmland soils. "Each year we lose tons of topsoil to our streams, lakes, and rivers," she said. "Acknowledging that state and federal funding alone can't meet our conservation demand for healthy soil and pollinator preservation, there is a push in the conservation community to engage the private sector so that we can scale this work up to where it needs to

be. The practice of pollinator-friendly solar will hold soils on-site and enrich them over time—making an incredibly productive use of the space today and into the future."

And there are functional and business benefits to the solar-design approach as well. The NREL in Golden, Colorado, estimates that site preparation costs for utility-scale solar projects account for 20 percent of utility-scale PV-installed costs. Reducing these costs via low-impact development can lead to cascading reductions in other environment-related costs and risks.

NREL's InSPIRE (Innovative Site Preparation and Impact Reductions on the Environment) study is developing a formal assessment of baseline costs, cost-reduction strategies, and environmental-impact-reduction strategies for ground-mounted PVs. Pollinator-friendly site development, along with other approaches to colocate solar and agricultural production and benefits, is one of the low-impact approaches being studied with several state-based project partners, including Clif Bar, NASA, University of Arizona, Organic Valley, University of Minnesota,

President Jimmy Carter's solar farm, Denison University, and several others.

Embracing innovation and committing to use ecological landscape design to stack additional benefits into solar development is a positive sign that solar industry leaders are working to avoid negative trade-offs that can accompany rapid growth.

*Rob Davis is the director of the Center for Pollinators in Energy at Fresh Energy. He helps accelerate the nation's transition to the use of clean and renewable energy. Davis's talk on pollinator-friendly solar, "This Unlikely 1960s Space Tech Can Help Save the Bees," is online at TED.com. Along with a senior analyst from NREL, Davis is cochair of the research and outreach committee for NREL's study into low-impact and pollinator-friendly solar-development approaches. Previously, Davis helped launch technology start-ups and created the international crowdsourced campaign that launched the Firefox web browser. He is a graduate of Macalester College.*

## Acknowledgments

Thank you to the editorial team at Princeton Architectural Press—Jennifer Lippert, Jan Hartman, and Kristen Hewitt—for their commitment to the book concept and thoughtful collaboration; Paul Wagner and Paula Baver, for their fantastic book design; and to the entire team at PAP.

Landscape designer and artist Walter Hood and landscape architect Björk Guðmundsdóttir provided the inspiration for *Good Energy*—Walter, through his Solar Strand, and Björk, through her lecture on the design of renewable energy in Iceland at the ASLA Conference on Landscape Architecture. I am grateful they were so gracious to contribute to *Good Energy*.

Gratitude to Mark Z. Jacobson and Rob Davis, who were very generous in sharing their ideas, research, and incredible positivity.

This book also could not have happened without the very busy project designers, clients, and developers who answered my many questions and explained how things like heat pumps and chilled beams work, reviewed drafts, and corrected errors. Peter Reynolds, Mick Pearce, Jim Palmer, Jim Cutler, Nicholas Pevzner, and Jonathan Davis—thank you for taking extra time to demystify things.

I am grateful to the photographers who granted me permission to use their excellent images, which make these projects come alive—Martine Hamilton Knight, Marion Brenner, Ariel Huber, and Nic Lehoux.

To Dena Kennett, Susan Cahill, Les Blackmore, Cecile and Tom Warnock, Marcia Diehl, Michael Higdon, Maria Bellalta, Jean Senechal Biggs, Ian Dillon, Paul Azzolini, and Dana Davidsen, thanks for always asking the dreaded question: How is the book going?

Thank you to my parents for buying me all those books.

# Selected Bibliography

Architecture 2030. "New Buildings: Embodied Carbon." https://architecture2030.org/new-buildings-embodied/.

Becque, Renilde, Debbie Weyl, Emma Stewart, Eric Mackres, Luting Jin, Xufei Shen. "Accelerating Building Decarbonization: Eight Attainable Policy Pathways to Net Zero Carbon Buildings for All." World Resources Institute, September 2019.

Caradonna, Jeremy L. *Sustainability: A History*. Oxford University Press, 2014.

City of Helsinki. "The Carbon-Neutral Helsinki 2035 Action Plan."

City of Melbourne. "Climate Change Mitigation Strategy to 2050."

European Commission. "Energy Efficient Buildings." https://ec.europa.eu/energy/topics/energy-efficiency/energy-efficient-buildings_en.

Green, Jared. "A New Park Where There Was Once a Canal," *The Dirt*, American Society of Landscape Architects, December 4, 2012, https://dirt.asla.org/2012/12/04/in-d-c-a-canal-becomes-a-park/.

Green, Jared. "Gina McCarthy: Keep up the Fight against Climate Change." *The Dirt*, American Society of Landscape Architects. November 17, 2019 https://dirt.asla.org/2019/11/17/gina-mccarthy-dont-give-up-in-the-fight-against-climate-change/

Green, Jared. "In Copenhagen, You Can Ski Down This Power Plant." *The Dirt*, American Society of Landscape Architects, February 21, 2019, https://dirt.asla.org/2019/02/21/in-copenhagen-you-can-ski-down-this-power-plant/

Hall, Dale, Hongyan Cui, and Nic Lutsey. "Electric Vehicle Capitals: Accelerating the Global Transition to Electric Drive." International Council on Transportation on Clean Transportation, October 2018

Hall, Dale, Hongyan Cui, Nic Lutsey. "Electric vehicle capitals of the world: What markets are leading the transition to electric?" International Council on Transportation on Clean Transportation, November 2017

Hawken, Paul. *Drawdown: The Most Comprehensive Plan Ever Proposed to Reverse Global Warming*. Penguin Books, 2017.

Höhne, Niklas, Michel den Elzen, Joeri Rogelj, Bert Metz, Taryn Fransen, Takeshi Kuramochi, Anne Olhoff, Joseph Alcamo, Harald Winkler, Sha Fu, Michiel Schaeffer, Roberto Schaeffer, Glen P. Peters, Simon Maxwell, Navroz K. Dubash. "Emissions: World Has Four Times the Work or One-Third of the Time." *Nature*, Vol 579. 5 March 2020. 25–28

Inman, Mason. "Going 'All The Way' with Renewable Energy?" *National Geographic*, January 16, 2011.

Intergovernmental Panel on Climate Change (IPCC). *Global Warming of 1.5° C: An IPCC Special Report on the Impacts of Global Warming of 1.5 °C Above Pre-Industrial Levels and Related Global Greenhouse Gas Emission Pathways, in the Context of Strengthening the Global Response to the Threat of Climate Change, Sustainable Development, and Efforts to Eradicate Poverty*. IPCC, 2018

Jacobson, Mark Z., Mark A. Delucchi. "A Path to Sustainable Energy by 2030." *Scientific American*, November 2009, 58–65

Jacobson, Mark Z., Mark A. Delucchi, Zack A.F. Bauer, Jingfan Wang, Eric Weiner, Alexander S. Yachanin. "100% Clean and Renewable Wind, Water, and Sunlight All-Sector Energy Roadmaps for 139 Countries of the World," *Joule 1*, Joule, September 6, 2017, 108-121.

Jacobson, Mark Z., Mark A. Delucchi, Mary A. Cameron, Brian V. Mathiesen. "Matching Demand with Supply at Low Cost in 139 Countries among 20 World Regions with 100% Intermittent Wind, Water, and Sunlight (WWS) for All Purposes." *Renewable Energy*, 123 (2018): 236–248

Kelley, Colin P., Shahrzad Mohtadi, Mark A. Cane, Richard Seager, Yochanan Kushnir. "Climate change in the Fertile Crescent and implications of the recent Syrian drought," *Proceedings of the National Academy of Sciences of the United States of America*, March 17, 2015, 3241-3246.

Leung, Jessica. "Decarbonizing U.S. Buildings." The Center for Climate and Energy Solutions. July 2018

Loring, Pamela H., Peter W.C. Paton, James D. McLaren, Hua Bai, Ramakrishna Janaswamy, Holly F. Goyert, Curtice R. Griffin, Paul R. Sievert. "Tracking Offshore Occurrence of Common Terns, Endangered Roseate Terns, and Threatened Piping Plovers with VHF Arrays." U.S. Department of the Interior, Bureau of Ocean Energy Management, Office of Renewable Energy Programs, April 2019

McCann, Jennifer et al. "Rhode Island Ocean Special Area Management Plan." Rhode Island Coastal Resources Management Council. October 19, 2010

Solar Strand. *Smart Policies for a Changing Climate*. American Society of Landscape Architects, 2019, https://climate.asla.org/SolarStrand.html

Tollefson, Jeff. "The Hard Truths of Climate Change—by the Numbers." Nature, September 19, 2019, 326-330." *Nature*. Vol 573. 19 September 2019. 326-330.

World Bank. "The Cost of Air Pollution: Strengthening the Economic Case for Action." World Bank Institute for Health Metrics and Evaluation, 2016, https://openknowledge.worldbank.org/handle/10986/25013

# Index

Page references for illustrations appear in *italics*

56 Brewing, 227
100% Earth: A vision for the transition to 100% wind, water & solar energy (The Solutions Project), 24
100.org, 19
100 percent Clean, Renewable Energy Movement, 19
"100 percent Clean and Renewable Wind, Water, and Sunlight All Sector-Energy Roadmaps for 139 Countries in the World" (Jacobson), 27
2009 World Games, Kaohsiung, Taiwan, *138*, 139, *139*

## A

A2F Architects, 222
Accord Passive House, Accord, New York, United States (Reynolds), *54*, *55*, *56*, *57*, *58*, *59*
Adlouni, Wassim, *108*, 109–10, *110*, *111*, *112*, *113*
Ahrentzen, Sherry, 45
Alibaba, 135
Almond, William, 181
Alstom Wind
  Haliade 150-6 MW turbines, 207, *207*
Amager Bakke (CopenHill), Copenhagen, Denmark (Ingels, Babcock & Wilcox Vølund), 15, *117*, *122*, *123*, *124*, *125*, *126*, *127*
Amager Resource Center (ARC), Copenhagen, Denmark, 123, *127*
American Bird Conservancy, United States, 205
  Bird-Smart Wind Energy Campaign, 208
American Recovery and Reinvestment Act of 2009, United States, 71
American Society of Landscape Architects (ASLA), United States, 123, 149
American Solar Grazing Association, United States, *228*

American Wind Energy Association, United States, *33*
America's Electrical Cooperatives, United States, 211
Anacostia Waterfront Corporation, Washington, DC, United States, 121
ARC. *See* Amager Resource Center (ARC), Copenhagen, Denmark
Archer-Wills, Anthony, 50, 51, 52, 53
Architecture 2030, 16–17, 174
Arkís, 222
ASLA. *See* American Society of Landscape Architects (ASLA), United States
Atelier Dreiseitl, 78, 79–80, *80*, *81*
*At Home with Autism: Designing Housing for the Spectrum* (Ahrentzen, Steele), 45
aurora borealis, *220*
Avasara Academy, Lavale, India (Case Design, Purushothaman), 15–16, *142*, *160*, *161*, 161–62, *162*, *163*, *164*, *165*
Avasara Leadership Institute, Lavale, India, 161

## B

Babcock & Wilcox Vølund, *122*, *123*, *124*, *125*, *126*, *127*
Bach, Malene, *163*
Barcelona, Spain, *6*, *7*
Barclay, Samuel, *161*, *162*
Bare Honey, Saint Joseph, Minnesota, United States, 227, *227*
Bee the Change, Vermont, United States, 227
Belfield Townhomes, Philadelphia, Pennsylvania, United States (Onion Flats), 37, *64*, *65*, *66*, *67*, *68*–*69*
Bhutan, 21, 202
*Biological Conservation*, 205
bioplastics, 61, 62
Bioregional, development firm, United Kingdom, 76
Birt, Arlene, *230*

Block Island Wind Farm, Block Island, Rhode Island, United States (Deepwater Wind), 203, *204*, *205*, *206*, *207*, 207–8, *209*
*Bloomberg*, 123
Bloomberg New Energy Finance, 129
Blueprint, *88*, *89*, *90*, *91*, *91*, *92*, *93*
BOEM. *See* US Department of the Interior
Brock Environmental Center, Virginia Beach, Virginia, United States (SmithGroup), 175, *180*, 181, *181*, *182*, *183*, *184*, *185*
Bullitt Center, Seattle, Washington, United States (Miller Hull Partnership), 16, 175, *186*, *187*, *187*–*88*, *189*
Bullitt Foundation, 187, 188

## C

California, *30*, *31*, 37, 174, 202
Cameron, Mary A., 27
Canal Park Development Association (CPDA), Washington, DC, United States, 121
Capitol Riverfront Business Improvement District, Washington, DC, United States, 121
Carmel Partners, 39, 40
Carter, Jimmy, *7*, 231
Case Design, *160*, *161*, 161–62, *162*, *163*, *164*, *165*
Caspari, Laura, 229
CBF. *See* Chesapeake Bay Foundation (CBF), United States
CDC. *See* Centers for Disease Control and Prevention (CDC), United States
Center for Climate and Energy Solutions, United States, 12–13, 174
Centers for Disease Control and Prevention (CDC), United States, 45
Centre for Interactive Research on Sustainability (CIRS) at the University of British Columbia, Vancouver, British Columbia, Canada (Perkins and Will), 143

CEO. *See* Colorado Energy Office (CEO), Colorado, United States
CH2. *See* Council House 2 (CH2), Melbourne, Australia (Pearce, DesignInc)
Chesapeake Bay Foundation (CBF), United States, 175, *180*, 181, *181*, *182*, 183, *184*, *185*
Chevron Energy Partners, 39
*China Daily*, 135
Christophers, John, *94*, 95, *96*, *97*, 98–99
CIRS. *See* Centre for Interactive Research on Sustainability (CIRS) at the University of British Columbia, Vancouver, British Columbia, Canada
Clever, 129, *133*
Clif Bar & Company, *230*, 231
Clif Family Winery, 227
climate-action movement, 14, 19, 142
climate change. *See* renewable energy
Climate Policy Initiative, 13
COBE, *128*, 129, *130*, *131*, *132*, *133*
Code for Sustainable Homes, United Kingdom, 95
Cogil, Cindy, 183
Colorado Energy Office (CEO), Colorado, United States, 211
Colorado School of Mines, Golden, Colorado, United States, 211
commercial, governmental, institutional buildings, 174–99
Conference on Landscape Architecture (2019), 14
Connecticut Residence, Connecticut, United States (Cutler), 37, 50, *51*, *52*, *53*
Connexus Energy, 227
Copher, Cage, *83*, *84*
Council House 2 (CH2), Melbourne, Australia (Pearce, DesignInc), 175, *194*, 195–96, *196*, *197*, *198*, *199*
COVID-19 pandemic, 13, 17, 37, 155, 174, 188, 195

# Image Credits

Published by
Princeton Architectural Press
202 Warren Street
Hudson, New York 12534
www.papress.com

ISBN 978-1-61689-909-7

Editor: Kristen Hewitt
Designers: Paul Wagner, Paula Baver

Library of Congress Control Number: 2020946846